W9-CEZ-720

THE EGG MARKETING BOARD

THE EGG MARKETING BOARD

A CASE STUDY OF MONOPOLY AND ITS SOCIAL COSTS

**THOMAS BORCHERDING
WITH GARY W. DOROSH**

THE FRASER INSTITUTE

1981

Canadian Cataloguing in Publication Data

Borcherding, Thomas, 1939-
    The Egg Marketing Board

    (Fraser Institute agricultural economics series)
    Bibliography: p.
    Includes index.
    ISBN 0-88975-019-X (pbk.)

    1. British Columbia. Egg Marketing Board.
2. Canadian Egg Marketing Agency. 3. Egg trade—
British Columbia—Costs. 4. Eggs—Prices—
British Columbia. I. Dorosh, Gary, 1942-
II. Fraser Institute (Vancouver, B.C.) III. Title.
IV. Series.
HD9284.C33B7   338.1'775'09711   C81-091104-3

Contents

Acknowledgements

We have been helped in great measure by the cooperation of Mr. Bill Wood, former head of the B.C. Poultry Division of the British Columbia Egg Marketing Board's office, in determining various facts about the federal and provincial egg boards' operations. Messrs. Frank J. Hammel, Jr., J.M. Kitterman, and Gary F. Strohmaier of the U.S. Department of Agriculture, Washington (State), Crop and Livestock Reporting Service in Seattle, were most kind in helping us discover Washington State egg prices; Maryon Brechin, former president of the Consumers' Association of Canada (CAC) sent us several documents that were useful, as did James Forbes of the University of British Columbia. Professor Forbes was generous to us with his time and made his extensive researches on the Canadian Egg Marketing Agency (CEMA) and the materials on which he based them, freely available to us.

Rhoda Borcherding typed a first draft, cheerfully, adding useful comments that only one could provide who is well-experienced in the ways of household production and informed by countless not always scintillating discussions with both eminent and yeoman level economists at numberless (she says numbing) social gatherings over a decade.

We presented our preliminary findings in the form of a

seminar to the Applied Economic Research Workshop at Simon Fraser University in September 1977. The chairman of that group, Herbert Grubel, his students and faculty colleagues, particularly Donald F. Gordon, Jack Knetsch, Peter Kennedy, Richard Schwindt, and Clyde Reed, provided pertinent suggestions then and later. Useful comments on a second draft were also made by Yoram Barzel of the University of Washington, John Berry of the [Canadian] Anti-Inflation Board, Stephen Ferris of Carleton University (Ottawa), and Michael Trebilcock, Faculty of Law, University of Toronto.

In addition, I am particularly indebted to discussions with and/or comments offered by Levis Kochin of the University of Washington, John McManus of Carleton University, and Richard Albion of the Australian National University. Professor Kochin's paper "Monopoly Profits and Social Losses," *Research in Law and Economics* (forthcoming 1981), given as a seminar at Simon Fraser University in Spring 1977, served as a model for the approach we took in Chapter III.

Not the least helpful was Michael Walker, Director of the Fraser Institute, who encouraged us in a number of ways and, on two occasions, uncovered useful information that otherwise would have been unavailable to us. Ann Popein, Laurie Hustler, and Kathy Hay of the Fraser Institute speedily, accurately, and efficiently typed several draft copies from progressively less legible and cryptic alterations of their previously immaculate efforts. Famah Andrew of Stanford's Graduate School of Business typed the final copy. Its cost was borne by the Hoover Institution, who in other ways also aided our efforts.

The work for this study was largely finished in December 1978, but other obligations prevented its completion at that time. Since then the Agricultural Economics Research Council of Canada has published *The Cost of Canada's Egg System* (January 1979). This work corroborates ours in the main and, if anything, suggests we were too conservative in Chapters II and III. Unfortunately, for the lack of time, we have been unable to incorporate much of its supportive findings in our study.

Finally, let us absolve all those who helped in our study from all error. Any that remains is our burden.

Vancouver   Thomas E. Borcherding

Preface

I. INTRODUCTION
The marketing board as cartel
One of the most notable aspects of agricultural policy in Canada during recent years has been the activity of marketing boards. Originally put in place to remove boom and bust cycles from the markets for agricultural products, and to ensure producers a "fair" return, marketing boards have become a highly politicized conduit for the transfer of income from consumers to producers. The extent to which marketing boards transfer income depends on their ability to maintain the price for the product at a higher level than would prevail in a free market. Marketing boards, like any cartel, are able artificially to maintain prices above the free market level by restricting the supply of the product available to the market. Unlike ordinary cartels which arise spontaneously from time to time and are usually illegal, marketing boards are usually encouraged and sanctioned by government and their powers therefore have the force of law.

Cartel membership—the quota
In general, cartels restrict the supply of their product by splitting up the market amongst their members. They do this

by granting quotas to their members. These quotas entitle the holder to produce and sell some particular amount of the product. To become a member of the cartel, a producer must acquire a quota.

If a marketing board (cartel) is successful—i.e., confers benefits on its members—it will be under constant pressure to accept new members. However, if the marketing board is "mature," new quotas will only be issued to provide new production to meet growth in the whole market. As a consequence, new entrants to the market can only produce the product for sale at the controlled price (become a member of the cartel) if they purchase a quota from an existing member. Accordingly, the pressure of potential producers who are not members to join the cartel is reflected in the price that must be paid for a quota.

A high market price for a quota implies that the marketing board is successful and does convey substantial benefits (income) on its members. A low or zero price would reflect the fact that potential producers do not regard membership in the cartel as having any value. It follows from this that the market price of a quota can be used as an indicator of the extent to which the marketing board does confer a benefit on its members.

Egg marketing boards

In this study, Professor Thomas Borcherding has applied this principle to estimate the extent to which the British Columbia Egg Marketing Board transfers income from consumers to producers. In the course of his work, Professor Borcherding develops the principles of an analytical framework that can be applied to marketing boards in general and therefore his work is valuable in a broader context. It is also valuable because it clearly identifies the real cost of a marketing board and provides signal warning of the consequences of extending the power of marketing boards over other products. The Fraser Institute is publishing this study to document the consequences of marketing boards and to stimulate public discussion of the economic issues at stake.

The economic issues associated with marketing boards are significant. Currently about 60 percent of total agricultural output in Canada is under the control of some federal or provincial board. Thus, although the particular impact of cartelized egg prices may have a modest effect on the consumer, the overall impact of boards on the total consumer budget may be quite large. For example, in a previous Fraser Institute study, *The Real Cost of the B.C. Milk Board*, it was established that the effect of the milk cartel was to maintain B.C. milk prices at a level higher than any other part of North America and some 13 percent higher than they would be in a free market. Recent estimates suggest that this continues to be true.

II. THE BRITISH COLUMBIA EGG MARKETING BOARD IN 1980

In his study, Professor Borcherding applied the analytical apparatus he develops to the operations of the B.C. Egg Marketing Board during 1975. He did this so he could compare his results to those obtained in other independent studies. The results of this comparison indicate that the Borcherding method of analysis is quite conservative in its assessment of the costs imposed on consumers by the operation of marketing boards. In fact, Borcherding's estimates are low by comparison with other estimates that have been made by academic and other professional investigators.

It is particularly interesting, therefore, to observe the estimates that emerge from applying Borcherding's analysis to the current circumstances in British Columbia. His analysis, updated by The Fraser Institute, suggests that by the end of 1980 the egg marketing cartel was imposing an extra cost of 21.0 cents per dozen on British Columbia consumers. In other words, consumers were paying for 14 eggs and receiving only a dozen.

This updated calculation is based on even more conservative assumptions than Borcherding used to arrive at his estimate. The basis of the new calculation is a quota value of

$1,956 per case. The actual price of quota ranged as high as $3,000 in 1980 but this figure may not be representative. A figure of $2,700 seems to be a reasonable average quota trading value for 1980. In order to make comparisons with the 1975 calculations, it is necessary to further reduce the $2,700 figure to account for the inflation that has elapsed in the interval (i.e. from 1975 to 1979). The inflation adjustment yields a quota value of $1,956 per case.

Many explanations are given by marketing board defenders as to why farmers are willing to pay such high prices for quota—i.e. for the right to produce eggs. Professor Borcherding maintains that the existence of profits above and beyond those which could be earned in a free egg market is the chief explanation. The investment in quota can be justified because it is a profitable investment. By observing how much farmers are willing to invest to purchase a single quota right and assuming the percentage return they would be satisfied with, we can infer how much extra profit farmers can earn by buying an extra quota right.

Defenders of the marketing board claim that the quota values are artificially high because many people who buy them, particularly foreigners, are satisfied with much lower rates of return than existing farmers can accept. The importance of this point can be seen by observing the following example. Suppose that the quotas were expected to last for only one year. Further assume that the marketing board was successful in maintaining prices 21 cents per dozen above the free market price. Now, if a prospective purchaser of quota required a return of 10 percent on the money invested in the quota, he or she would pay a maximum of 19.1 cents for the right to produce one dozen eggs. The difference is explained by the fact that the 19.1 cents invested at 10 percent would grow to 21 cents by the end of the year.

If, on the other hand, an investor expected a return of only 5 percent on the investment in quota, he or she would pay as much as 20 cents per dozen for the right to produce eggs.

This difference between what people would be willing to pay rises as the expected life of the quota increases. For example, if the marketing board and hence the quota, were expected to last for 7 years and the excess profits were expected to remain at 21.0 cents per dozen, a person seeking a 5 percent return would pay $64.72 for the right to produce a dozen eggs, whereas a person requiring a 10 percent return would pay only $55.73.

The implication is that, as is claimed by the defenders of the marketing board, the high value of quota may to some extent reflect either excess profits in egg production or unrealistically low (i.e. less than current market) interest rate requirements on the part of some investors. If the latter is true then the amount of excess profit accruing to the industry may be lower than is inferred on the basis of current market interest rates. However, as is clear from the example, the effect of assuming a very low (5 percent) discount rate is swamped by the overall magnitudes involved. Whichever interest rate is assumed, we find that because of the excess profit available, the bid price for quota will be quite high.

In order to explicitly take these possibilities into account, we have calculated the implied excess profit figure of 21 cents per dozen using an interest rate of 5 percent and assuming that quota enforcement will last for at least 7 years. In other words, the 21 cents excess cost per dozen ought to be regarded as a minimum estimate since it employs the most conservative of a wide range of possible assumptions. While this figure stands on its own as a scientific inference, it is worth noting that inter-regional comparisons could support numbers much higher than 21 cents per dozen.

For example, a comparison between egg prices in Vancouver and those prevailing in Washington State (which does not have a marketing board with the power to set prices), clearly supports a much higher excess profit figure. The best consumer buy (excluding "loss leaders" and "specials") in Vancouver at the end of 1980 was $1.35 per dozen Grade A extra large eggs. In Seattle the price was $1.04 per dozen in

Canadian dollar terms.[1] As Borcherding's careful analysis of the historical relationship shows, this large and widening differential between egg prices in the two cities has existed ever since the B.C. Egg Marketing Board was established in 1968.

Production efficiency losses

One of the reasons prices are higher in B.C. is that the effect of the Egg Marketing Board is to keep the average size of B.C. egg farms below their optimal size. This results from the ruling that farms may not produce more than a certain number of cases of eggs per week (unless they were doing so before the establishment of the marketing board). The fact that their output is limited effectively means that farms cannot exceed a certain size and cannot grow to take advantage of the various efficiencies and cost reductions that large scale operations can provide. Again, the comparison between B.C. egg markets and those in Washington State is very instructive and explains why a large price differential will continue to exist between the two areas. In Washington State about 66 percent of annual egg production is derived from farms having flocks larger than 50,000 birds, in B.C. only 5 percent of total egg production comes from such farms. More importantly, in B.C. 66 percent of egg production is derived from flocks which range in size from 10,000 to 50,000 birds. According to a report done for the Canadian Egg Marketing Agency this is the least cost efficient production range. Both smaller flocks (12,000 birds or less) and larger flocks (more than 48,000 birds) experience lower production costs. The mid-range farms, so prevalent in B.C., experienced costs 8 percent higher than small farms and 16 percent higher than large farms.

---

1. The actual standard supermarket price in Seattle was 91 cents for "jumbos," 86 cents for extra large, 82 cents for AA large, 81 cents for medium, and 61 cents for small. In order to make the comparison these were adjusted to Canadian dollar terms using an exchange rate of $1 U.S. for $1.176 Canadian.

RRECTION: Second paragraph, line 5, should read as follows:
80 cases* of eggs

III. POLICY IMPLICATIONS

The consumer interest

The alleged objectives of marketing boards are to protect the consumer from erratic price movements and to encourage and protect the family farm. This study shows that the costs to consumers and the producing sector of such worthy intentions is relatively high in practice. The current overall cost to society in terms of waste is roughly equivalent to smashing two eggs from every dozen produced.

As the study makes clear, the process of discovering this actual social cost of the operation of the egg cartel is very complex and, as a consequence, is not generally known to consumers. If there were a weekly public destruction of 10,680 dozen eggs (the actual loss incurred), the public would probably be less tolerant of this government-sponsored intervention in the egg production process and demand an alternative arrangement. The fact that the loss is hidden in higher egg prices and because the cost to individual consumers is low—about 20 or so dollars per year—means that consumers have no real incentive to collectively pressure government to end the cartelization of egg production.

Moreover, the marketing board can, because of this lack of information and incentive go on claiming that it operates in the consumer interest. Borcherding's analysis clearly shows, however, that it is farmer interests and not those of consumers which are served by marketing boards.

The producer interest

The extent to which marketing boards protect the interest of new farmers is also called into question by Borcherding's analysis. In order to become an egg farmer and be able to sell eggs via the egg marketing cartel, a young person must buy into the cartel by purchasing quota from an existing member. The cost of doing so for even the smallest viable farm would today in British Columbia, cost about $300,000—a figure far in excess of the total costs (birds, buildings, etc.)—involved in actually producing the eggs. Evidently, egg marketing boards don't protect the interests of new farmers. But they obviously are supporting the interests of existing farmers and those who stand to reap a handsome benefit when they decide to leave the industry.

What to do about the marketing board

In his conclusions, Professor Borcherding is reluctant to recommend the abandonment of the current egg board although all of the economic analysis points in that direction. His reluctance is based on the view that consumers may be willing to pay the cost of marketing boards because of some indefinable social benefits that may accrue from the subsidies they provide to small farmers. He does point out, however, that marketing boards are a very inefficient way in which to provide the subsidy—the additional social cost of transferring each dollar is about 50 cents. Because of these large on-going costs, Borcherding strongly suggests that alternatives, such as direct subsidies to "worthy" farmers, be considered and that marketing boards be phased out via some form of quota buy-back scheme. His latter suggestion is motivated by the fact that farmer resistance, in the form of political lobbying, would be much less severe if some form of compensation were provided.

As noted above, we are confident that if consumers really appreciated the costs of marketing boards, their expression of dissatisfaction would drown out the self-interested clamour from those producers who benefit from marketing boards. In the interest of better informing consumers about the nature of these costs, The Fraser Institute has been pleased to support and publish Professor Borcherding's analysis. However, owing to the fact that he has independently arrived at his conclusions, they may or may not conform to the views of the members of The Fraser Institute.

Michael A. Walker
January, 1981

The interest of the dealers . . . in any particular branch of trade or manufactures, is always in some respect different from, and even opposite to, that of the public. To widen the market and to narrow the competition is always the interest of the dealers. To widen the market may frequently be agreeable enough to the interest of the public; but to narrow the competition must always be against it, and can serve only to enable the dealers, by raising their profits above what they naturally would be, to levy, for their own benefit, an absurd tax upon the rest of their fellow citizens. The proposal of any new law or regulation of commerce which comes from this order, ought always to be listened to with great precaution, and ought never to be adopted till after having been long and carefully examined, not only with the most scrupulous, but with the most suspicious attention. It comes from an order of men, whose interest is never exactly the same with that of the public, who have generally an interest to deceive and even to oppress the public, and who accordingly have, upon many occasions, both deceived and oppressed it.

Adam Smith, *An Inquiry into the Nature and the Causes of the Wealth of Nations*

THE AUTHORS

Thomas E. Borcherding received his B.A. (High Honours) from the University of Cincinnati in 1961 and his Ph.D. from Duke University in 1966. He is now Professor of Economics at Simon Fraser University in Burnaby, British Columbia, and has just returned from sabbatical leave at the Hoover Institution, Stanford University. He has also served on the faculty of the University of Washington, Virginia Polytechnic Institute and State University, and the University of Toronto. He has, in the past, been a post-doctoral fellow at University of Virginia's Thomas Jefferson Center for Study in Political Economy and in 1974-75 at the Hoover Institution. Professor Borcherding has been a member of the Board of Editors for the *Canadian Journal of Economics* and has published in that and many other leading journals. He now serves as co-editor of *Economic Inquiry*, the journal of the Western Economic Association. He edited and contributed several essays to *Budgets and Bureaucrats: The Sources of Government Growth* (Durham, North Carolina: Duke University Press, 1977). At present his research is devoted to the questions of public spending growth, bureaucracy, spending and taxation limits, the economics of public enterprise, compensation for public takings of private property, and various issues in the theory of markets, externalities, and collective goods.

Gary W. Dorosh received his B.A. from Simon Fraser University in 1973 and his M.A. in 1975. Since 1974 he has taught economics and quantitative methods at Douglas College in New Westminster, British Columbia. He is co-author with Peter Kennedy of *Dateline Canada: Understanding Economics through Press Reports* (Scarborough, Ontario: Prentice-Hall of Canada Ltd., 1978). He began the study of egg marketing boards in British Columbia with "The British Columbia Egg Marketing Board: A Critical Evaluation" (extended essay for the M.A. degree, Department of Economics and Commerce, Simon Fraser University, August 1975).

Introduction

The study of eggs in British Columbia may seem to many Canadian and other readers a trivial matter to consider, especially in a world where inflation causes prices to double in a decade, where macroeconomic instability and other market distortions for whatever reason cause one of every twelve persons in the Canadian workforce to declare himself or herself unemployed, where government claims almost half the GNP and supplies goods and services that absorb nearly two-fifths of national output, where energy crises continue, and other Third World commodity cartels may soon impose noticeable losses in living standards. Yet all these problems at their heart are problems in coordinating exchange, production, and distribution and in establishing who has the right to do what, with which, to whom, where, and at what time. These are basically problems in social choice and involve the use and often redirection and/or suppression of competitive forces. We submit that the Canadian egg marketing scheme has this last characteristic in common with these more momentous social problems. The study of one small sample of public intervention for suppression of competition helps us to understand the grander restrictions, if only because the former is so much more manageable in scope.

1

Although eggs constitute a very minor fraction of the average Canadian household's food budget, and a trivial fraction of its total income, what has happened (and is happening) in this market has wider meaning. This market is characterized by severe restraints imposed not by natural market forces of scale economies from the use of a specialized, capital-intensive technology or from limited information, but by the very visible hand of state intervention. As such it serves as an exemplar of a large number of other highly regulated activities in the Canadian economy. To the extent that the lessons drawn from this miniscule activity have informational spillovers onto the larger question of agricultural policy and the still more important issue of competitive restrictions via quotas, regulatory impediments, and tariffs, the issues raised have consequences beyond the Lilliputian contribution of eggs to our rich economy.

The plan of our study is as follows: in Chapter I we briefly discuss the history of the British Columbia Egg Marketing Board (hereafter the BCEMB) and its federal coordinator, the Canadian Egg Marketing Agency (CEMA). In Chapter II, we present evidence that competition has been severely restricted by these boards and that this has had a dramatic effect on the price of fresh (shell) eggs. Our third chapter attempts to measure the social cost of the monopoly created by these egg boards. A dollar figure is given for this damage as well as an estimate of the cost of these egg boards to consumers alone. Though we attempt in this chapter to be conservative in our calculations, the net losses are still a large fraction of the sales volume, equivalent to smashing one egg in every dozen sold to households in B.C. Still, the fuzzy nature of some of our data leads us to admit that, though more than a speculation, this loss figure should be thought of as a significant order of magnitude rather than a precise number.[1] We do not suggest, however, that these losses "prove" that the egg boards ought to be dismantled. That would involve too much scholarly *hubris*, since benefits may accrue that we have neglected or which the economist's cost-benefit methods might ignore. Rather, Chapter III gives only a social price tag. The "buyer," the general public and its not always diligent fiduciaries, the provincial and federal legislatures, can decide if other utilities offset this cost sufficiently to warrant their continued "purchase." Unfortunately, the nature of social cost measurements requires use of the economist's more technical tools. These can be passed over by the unannointed much as we all do when we read technical studies in engineering and science purporting to establish certain hypotheses concerning health, product safety and durability, and environmental impacts. The thorny question of policy is discussed in Chapter IV, where alternatives to the current egg marketing scheme are also considered.

Chapter I
A Brief Description

But though the law cannot hinder people of the same trade from sometimes assembling together, it ought do nothing to facilitate such assemblies; much less to render them necessary.
Adam Smith, *Wealth of Nations*

Currently in Canada there are more than one hundred provincial agricultural marketing boards. At least one (and usually seven or more) are found in each of the ten provinces.[2] Almost every type of commodity is covered, as Table I-1 indicates. In 1974 Professor James Forbes *et al.* calculated that between 40 and 60 percent of all Canadian agricultural output came under the control of some federal or provincial board and by the Fall of 1979, 60 percent was a more realistic estimate.[3]

Such attempts to intervene in the market for agriculture are not a recent phenomenon, however, but began with the Granger Movement in 1867 in the United States,[4] and crossed into Ontario in 1872.[5] Essentially, the Grange sought to protect its members from what it perceived were the monopolistic practices of two sellers of its important inputs, the railroads (transportation) and banks (mortgage money and other credit). Further, it wished to shield its membership from what it thought were the tactics of greedy middlemen,

5

6 *Egg Marketing Board*

Table I-1

Products Subject to Marketing Boards in Canada—1976
(number of boards in parentheses)

Province	Products
British Columbia	dairy, fruit, broilers, eggs, oysters, turkeys, potatoes, and certain other vegetables (11)
Alberta	grains, cattle, hogs, sheep and wool, dairy, turkeys, eggs and other fowl, potatoes and other vegetables (10)
Saskatchewan	hogs, sheep and wool, dairy, broilers, eggs, honey, turkeys (7)
Manitoba	grains, hogs, dairy, broilers, turkeys, eggs, fish, vegetables, honey (9)
Ontario	winter wheat, seed corn, soybeans, hogs, dairy, broilers, turkeys, eggs, fruits, vegetables, tobacco, dried beans, tomato seedlings (22)
Quebec	dairy, broilers and turkeys, eggs, blueberries, tomatoes, pulpwood, maple products, tobacco (26)
Nova Scotia	hogs, dairy, broilers, turkeys, eggs and pullets, tobacco, wool (7)
New Brunswick	hogs, dairy, broilers, eggs, turkeys, apples, bedding plants, pulpwood (10)
Prince Edward Island	hogs, dairy, broilers, eggs, potatoes and other vegetables, tobacco seed (8)
Newfoundland	eggs (1)

Source: The Bank of Nova Scotia: "Marketing Boards in Canada" with additions by John Berry of the (Canadian) Anti-Inflation Board.

the supposedly monopsonistic purchasers of its products (processors, packers, grain merchants, brokers, etc.). The Grange attempted to do this with stunning success in the U.S. Midwest by pressing for regulatory legislation of certain kinds restricting the powers of the railroads to set rates and of bankers to foreclose. They also undertook, without much success, the formation of voluntary cooperatives for buying and selling of their key inputs and produce as well as storing product for reasons of price stabilization.[6]

Marketing boards as such developed much later (1921), and not initially in the U.S. and Canada, but in Queensland, Australia.[7] In 1913, however, the tree fruit growers of the Okanagan Valley in British Columbia did form a selling co-op. Its members prospered, as did almost all B.C. farmers during World War I, but in 1920 it began to disintegrate, since it had no legal means to restrict product supply and entry of nonmembers into this market.[8] In 1923 another voluntary B.C. tree fruit co-op enlisted almost nine-tenths of these growers. Nonmembers refused to restrict their supply, however, and instead flooded the market with their produce. Of course, the co-op again failed.[9] These lessons taught by the self-interested actions of free riders were not lost on B.C. growers and their political representatives in Victoria. In 1927, the *B.C. Produce Marketing Act* was passed. Patterned after Australian legislation giving producers, via their elected committees of direction, power to set price and exact levies to accomplish price equalizations over time. Because of its actions, which were deemed to interfere with interprovincial trade and to constitute an indirect tax, the federal Supreme Court held the act *ultra vires*. A 1929 B.C. *Dairy Relief Act* also suffered legal death for the same reason.[10]

Difficulties in Canadian agriculture after World War I, but particularly in the Thirties, are well-known to every reader, be he or she familiar with Canadian economic history or not, since the Depression hardly exempted agriculture anywhere from its devastation. In 1934, the (Canadian) Royal Commission on Price Spreads blamed these conditions on "weak" marketing conditions and excessive concentration among processors and secondary industries.[11] Such commissions and diagnoses were common in those days all over the democratic world. The "treatment of choice" was typified by the New Deal restrictions created under the *U.S. Agriculture Adjustment Act* and the *National Recovery Act*, which held that the solution to massive market failure could be found in the creation of new monopolies to offset the market power of the monopolies that were presumed to exist already.[12]

The Price Spreads Commission's recommendations were of this genre and later took the legislated form of the *National Products Marketing Act* of 1934, which provided for a Dominion Marketing Board. The latter had the power to introduce sublevel boards for various commodities based on a majority assent of local producers. By the end of 1934 twenty boards existed, but this legislation was nullified in 1935 by the Supreme Court on the grounds that the federal government lacked the power to regulate intraprovincial trade.[13] Several of the provinces (beginning with B.C.'s *Natural Products Act* of 1936) then passed laws which permitted existing local boards to operate under provincial control. These were held constitutional, and all subsequent provincial and federal legislation is patterned after the 1936 B.C. act. By 1940, boards of some sort were found in all provinces save Quebec. The Canadian Wheat Board, created under 1935 legislation as a Crown corporation, did survive judicial scrutiny, since its policy was concerned almost entirely with exports, an area reserved to the federal government under the *British North America Act*.[14]

This legal pattern was traced almost exactly in the U.S., except that the judges there, to quote Mr. Dooley, "read the 'lection returns" more quickly, and the second *Agricultural Adjustment Act* of 1938 permitting massive government intervention into agriculture was sustained by the Supreme Court.[15] In Canada, however, World War II came in the Fall of 1939, and patriotism and the beginning of prosperity assuaged agricultural interests. Still, during the late Thirties many provincial boards were formed that survived legal attacks by the simple expedient of not *overtly* restricting interprovincial imports and exports. This meant, of course, that their powers were limited as far as affecting product prices and farm incomes. We would expect that through their powers to regulate quality, health, and safety some restrictions on entry of product from outside would have taken place, but we have no ready evidence on this.

In 1949, however, an *Agricultural Products Marketing Act* was passed by the federal government which permitted provincial boards to restrict interprovincial movements of products as well as exports. By the mid-1950s all but one of the ten provinces, Newfoundland, had passed laws whose scope was significantly broadened by this 1949 federal law.[16] Still later, Bill C-176, the *Farm Products Marketing Act* of 1972, was passed, permitting active cooperation among the provinces, nicely by-passing Section 121 of the *B.N.A. Act*, particularly with respect to restricting foreign imports and control of "dumping" by other provinces.[17] Among the causes of this development, if one is to believe the press, were the so-called "chicken and egg wars" involving Quebec, Manitoba, and Ontario.[18, 19]

During the period from the passage of the 1949 *Agriculture Products Marketing Act* until the debate over Bill C-176, producers argued that unless controls were national, provincial schemes that attempted to raise prices and incomes (as well as to stabilize them) would be largely ineffective. The 1972 Act created the National Farm Product Marketing Council (hereafter NFPMC) which was charged with coordinating, supervising, and reviewing the various national marketing boards' policies according to their view of the "public interest."[20] The mechanics of this law are simple. Producers apply to the NFPMC, a three- to nine-member Cabinet appointed group, through their provincial boards. If their plans are acceptable to the NFPMC, which must have a producer majority, it can sanction a largely self-governing, solely producer-controlled national coordinating board for the product.[21] So far it has approved and implemented CEMA and the Canadian Turkey Marketing Agency (1974). Creation of a national chicken broiler agency became a reality at the end of 1978.[22]

Four reasons are typically advanced to justify agricultural marketing boards, and in particular the BCEMB and CEMA. First, the nature of agriculture leads to great price uncertainties because of the seasonal and cyclical variabilities of demand and supply. Smoothing out price fluctuations is said to benefit both producers and consumers. Second, it is alleged that producer returns are often driven below those necessary to keep farmers in the industry. By stabilizing price and supply via regulatory fiat and restrictive quotas, consumers are said to benefit in the long run since, otherwise, the industry in question would contract and prices rise. A variant of this argument addresses instead the inequity of farmers receiving "inadequate" returns over time, compared to individuals in the other sectors of the economy. Third, the free market when left to its own devices drives out small producers and replaces them with the large, impersonal "agro-business." Marketing boards, by protecting the "family farm," preserve an allegedly important segment of the social order, the yeoman farmer. Finally, since marketing boards can standardize the terms of sale, superior quality and mutually superior contractual conditions emerge beyond what one would predict from unregulated marketings of the commodity.[23]

The mechanics of CEMA and BCEMB's respective operations are complex in detail, but without undue distortion they can be summarized in brief.

Membership in CEMA consists of twelve persons, one each appointed by the relevant marketing boards of each province and two named by the federal Cabinet for one- or two-year terms.[24] Decisions are often made *in camera*. CEMA sets a yearly national output figure and allocates it among the ten provincial boards. Prior to 1977 these were converted into cases, a unit consisting of 30 dozen eggs per week. Table I-2 lists the total marketing quotas each year set by CEMA since June 1973 and, before then, by the BCEMB acting on its own. Prior to 1977, quota was set in terms of numbers of eggs per week, but since then quota has been set in terms of maximum numbers of laying hens per unit of quota held. Adjustment for seasonal variation over the year is made each week by the BCEMB reducing the annual marketing quota as much as 25 percent at certain times. The actual average marketing quotas for B.C. are also given in Table I-2.[25]

Table I-2

Total Annual Marketing (TAM) and
Annual Marketing Quota (AMQ), 1968-1979

Year	Number of Producers	AMQ (cases per week)[a]	TAM (cases per week)[a]	% AMQ Marketed
1968	463	37,182	31,864	85.9
1969	418	37,604	33,477	89.0
1970	391	37,386	33,909	90.7
1971	362	37,487	34,315	91.5
1972	324	37,740	33,425	88.6
1973	272	36,462	31,367	86.0
1974	267	36,852	31,486	85.4
1975	227	36,228	30,978	85.5
1976	224	36,700	32,987	89.8
1977	217	36,700[b]	33,406	91.3
1978	198	36,700[b]	34,062	92.8
1979[c]	193	36,700	34,900	95.1

Source: *1968-1973 Summary of the Special Audit of Egg Production Quotas*, as issued by the B.C. Egg Marketing Board (April 1974). Data for 1974-1977 from minutes of Annual Meeting of the B.C. Egg Producers held in March or April. Data for 1978 via conversation with BCEMB officials.

[a]One case is 30 dozen.

[b]The 1977 and 1978 AMQ figures are estimates.

[c]Data for 1979 based on third quarter information provided by BCEMB in phone conversation.

Pricing, established by a complicated formula to be discussed in Part B of the next chapter, yields a provincial price to the farmer. Fresh eggs within quota, but in excess of what the "shell" egg market will absorb, are "broken out" and diverted to the domestic and international processed egg or "breaker" market, together with those eggs known as "cracks" or "seconds." Prices in the breaker market, consisting of liquid, powdered, and frozen eggs, are set by the free market.[26] To the producer, however, it is of no consequence whether his eggs within his quota go to the fresh or breaker market, since the registered receiving stations (graders) pay the provincial price for those eggs. Sharp penalties are assessed for eggs in excess of quota. A fund administered by CEMA and the provincial boards makes up the difference between the fresh and breaker prices. Revenues for this fund are derived by joint BCEMB and CEMA levies on producers for every dozen eggs sold.[27] When these funds become dangerously low or actually run negative balances, quota is readjusted downward and/or fees are raised. As a result, provincial quotas as set by CEMA and the split of levy fees between provincial boards and CEMA have been the subject of great contention in the past.[28]

The BCEMB, formed in July of 1967 and effectively in place in 1968, was the first provincial egg board in Canada. It is made up of four producers elected by its members with certain regional constraints.[29] Quotas specifying allowable output per farm were originally allocated according to the extent of the operation, measured in terms of flock size during the immediate past six months. (Since this formula was known well beforehand, it is alleged that flocks were increased before the six-month cut off date.) These quota rights were not originally intended to be directly transferable among producers, but only through sale of the farm.

This was changed in mid-1976, when quota rights could be sold "untied" to the farm where they were originally exercised, though constraints were placed on imports of quota rights to the Lower Mainland from Vancouver Island or the B.C. Interior.[30] Other restrictions were also placed on quota purchasers. Before 1977 no farm could hold more than 200 units of quota except for the 35 producers who had a greater number in 1967 when the B.C. scheme began.

In 1977, however, two things of interest happened at the behest of CEMA. First, the means of specifying quota was changed to include, in addition, the number of birds permitted per case.[31] This was considered necessary to ensure that provincial quotas were enforced and "leakages" plugged.

Second, and no less interesting, the BCEMB allowed the size of operations to increase from 200 units of quota and 14,000 adult birds to 280 units and 20,000 adult birds. Table I-2 indicates how the size of farms in terms of quota has increased since 1968, the first year of the BCEMB. The reader should note that the number of producers had declined by almost half, even before 1976, indicating that mergers were very common.

Many other fascinating details of the BCEMB and CEMA must necessarily be omitted, since space permits only a small fraction to be covered. However, we will assess evidence concerning one important question: whether or not the BCEMB and CEMA have followed their legislative mandate "to promote . . . efficient, and competitive producing and marketing . . . [with] due regard to the interests of producers and consumers." The issues involved are not inconsequential, since, in an early version, Competition Bill C-42 brought the actions of all marketing boards under its legislative scrutiny.[32] This version never received final reading, but was replaced by Bill C-13 (still pending ratification), which exempts marketing boards. CAC representatives and their friends assure us that proponents of freer agricultural markets will attempt to bring marketing boards under the ambit of future iterations of anti-combines legislation.

Chapter II
Evidence of Monopoly Power

To confer a monopoly upon a producer or dealer or upon a set of producers or dealers not too numerous to combine is to give them the power of levying any amount of taxation [sic] on the public for their individual benefit which will not make the public forego the use of the commodities.

John Stuart Mill, *Principles of Political Economy*

People of the same trade seldom meet together, even for merriment and amusement, but the conversation ends in a conspiracy against the public, or in some contrivance to raise prices.

Smith, *Wealth of Nations*

The effect, and often the purpose, of legal barriers to entry is to increase the wealth of those who were already in the market.

Armen Alchian and William R. Allen, *Exchange and Production: Competition, Coordination, and Control*

Several pieces of evidence will be offered to substantiate the hypothesis that the powers of supply control possessed by the BCEMB since 1968 and strengthened by CEMA in 1972 have been exercised to restrict the supply of fresh eggs below that which otherwise would have been forthcoming under a free market. The first is empirically casual, but is based on inferences from economic theory. The second and third are more empirically substantive, but they are based on studies that are hard for us to assess without a great deal more

14

information. The fourth is based on a comparison of the B.C. fresh egg market with a similar area, Washington State, where competitive conditions are generally thought to exist. The last piece, based upon positive quota values, is entirely persuasive, and we know of no sensible rival explanation that would be consistent with its finding other than the presence of monopoly power.

A. SOME CASUAL EVIDENCE

Economists tell us that, other things being equal, when the relative price of a product rises, less of it will be consumed. Since this "law of demand" is backed by overwhelming empirical evidence, we can employ it to test whether the relative price[33] of fresh eggs has risen in Canada because of an artificial restriction on supply. To do this we take the ratio, before and after CEMA, of per capita consumption of table grade eggs in Canada to that of the U.S. Implicitly, the argument offered here is that a major fraction of production costs in each country (probably more than four-fifths) depends on factors traded internationally, such as feed grain products and capital; hence, changes in cost in the one market ought to be, sooner or later, accompanied by roughly similar changes in the other. Further, changes in real incomes and "tastes," such as cholesterol consciousness, ought also to be similar, because of the massive economic, cultural, and informational interdependencies that exist between these two economies. Any change in the observed consumption ratios should reflect some difference in relative prices that are peculiar to the one or the other country.

The Food Prices Review Board calculated that in the pre-egg marketing board days of 1965, Canadian per capita egg consumption was 81 percent of that in the U.S. In 1971, still pre-CEMA but post-provincial board days, it had fallen, but only to 79 percent. By the end of 1973, however, and the first six months of CEMA's operation, that ratio had declined to 73 percent.[34]

While there might be other explanations, one possible reason for such a fall is that CEMA permitted a cartelization of the Canadian fresh egg market that provincial egg boards were unsuccessful in achieving on their own.

B. THE FORBES' STUDY FOR THE CONSUMERS' ASSOCIATION OF CANADA

On February 26, 1976, Professors James D. Forbes (University of British Columbia), Robert R. Kerton (University of Waterloo), and Daryl F. Kraft (University of Manitoba) presented a lengthy brief to the NFPMC in Ottawa on behalf of the Consumers' Association of Canada (CAC). Forbes *et al.* called for an 8 to 15 cent per dozen rollback on the price of Grade A large table eggs (depending on the province).

They argued that the various provincial egg boards, through their coordinating agent, CEMA, had developed a cost-of-production pricing formula which set shell prices far above that level which yielded "fair" (i.e., competitive) returns as mandated in the legislation that brought these provincial egg boards and CEMA into existence. These noncompetitive prices, they insisted, were maintained by strictly enforced provincial quotas and by import controls over and above that afforded by tariff protection.

It is not feasible in this section to review in detail the CEMA pricing formula, but the interested reader will find it discussed in the two documents commissioned by CEMA and produced in 1975 by P.S. Ross & Partners, a management consulting firm with Ottawa headquarters.[35] Essentially, the studies attempted to develop a model for pricing eggs based on production costs for the typical or representative farm that yields competitive returns. That data and methodological difficulties made the researchers' task difficult can be gleaned from the following paragraph from their first report:

> *The decisions involved in using cost of production information to establish or control market prices of producer support prices are essentially economic and political in nature and cannot be justified simply by reference to accounting principles.*[36]

This appears to us as another way of saying that (a)

measuring the social opportunity costs of egg production is very difficult, and (b) certain needs cannot be justified on the basis of market considerations alone. No serious student of Canadian egg boards should neglect this (dull but) important attempt to put egg board pricing policy on a "fair" but mechanically operational basis.[37]

Undaunted by P.S. Ross' warning, Forbes, Kerton, and Kraft attacked the two reports on an input by input basis. Without going into all the details of either the Ross/CEMA or Forbes/CAC calculations, let us compare their respective estimates for each input for the Province of Ontario in Table II-1.

It is impossible here, given constraints of space, to say nothing of competence, to discuss authoritatively each item

Table II-1

Cost of Production per Dozen of Grade A Large Eggs in Ontario, 1975

Item	Ross/CEMA[a] (cents)		Forbes/CAC[a] (cents)	
Feed	32.03		27.63	(28.46)
Labour	4.50		2.34	(3.94)
Pullets	10.76		11.82	(12.35)
Capital Depreciation	2.10		1.43	(1.50)
Overhead	4.61		3.55	(3.73)
Risk of Flock Destruction	.35		.01	(.35)
Return on Investment	2.10		1.53	(1.61)
Conversion to Grade A Large	5.45		5.00	
CEMA/Provincial Board Levies	5.00	(4.25)	1.75	
National Transportation Adjustments	2.10		0	
Wholesale Price	69.00	(66.15)	55.06	(58.69)
Differential:		13.94	(10.31)	

[a]From Forbes' testimony on behalf of the CAC in Ottawa, 26 February 1976 to the National Farm Marketing Council. Figures in parentheses are amended estimates submitted by Forbes and the CAC to this same group in Fredericton, New Brunswick, on 9 March 1976.

in Table II-1, but it is possible to give the reader a flavour of the Forbes/CAC attack on the Ross/CEMA formula with respect to two major items: feed and the CEMA/provincial boards' levies.

Feed costs per dozen eggs depend not only on the price of mash, but upon the assumed rate of lay. Forbes *et al.* presented evidence that, among other things, the Ross/CEMA feed-conversion ratio was excessive because the lay rate chosen was much too low. For example, they claimed that an excessive amount of time between a pullet's acquisition and the beginning of her egg laying was assumed. On the levy structure, the Forbes/CAC groups found the 2.5 cents for surplus removal to be totally unjustified, since it appeared to them as an implicit subsidy of the "breaker," or processed egg market.[38] Further, they argued that the remaining cost of administration was excessive, given the usual standards of "good business practices," by a factor of three or four times.[39] Their "competitive" levy, 1.75 cents, turns out to be the exact provincial level as of February 1976, a coincidence on which we cannot comment.[40]

Forbes himself also stated to the press at that time that B.C. egg prices were some 14.6 cents above normal costs of production plus what he called "reasonable levies" of 1.75 cents.[41] For B.C. he particularly took exception to what he called the "phantom transportation" charges of 10 cents that equalized B.C.'s and Manitoba's costs. According to the CEMA formula, Manitoba has a competitive advantage in fresh egg production. If eggs from that province were to sell in B.C. competitively with B.C. products, they would receive roughly the same price, but bear an added 10 cents per dozen in transport. Thus, B.C. producers must have 10 cents per dozen higher costs. Forbes points out elsewhere however, that only 3 percent of B.C.'s fresh eggs are supplied by Manitoba. The rest move only short distances within the province.[42]

Unfortunately, the question of appropriateness of formula to egg pricing is objectively difficult to assess. For instance, Max Roytenberg, CEMA's general manager, denied that prices were excessive and referred to Forbes' study as "academic speculation" and "figures picked out of the air."[43] Fairness would require him to admit that P.S. Ross' pricing formula is hardly different in its methodology, though Forbes' *et al.* approach appears to be drawn from a much smaller sample.[44] Of course, it is futile to argue over an "equitable" pricing formula in a world where cost efficient factor proportions shift because of technical change and innovation as well as input price changes. The ideal operation is not ascertainable *ex ante*, but only by scrutinizing the "survivors." Since competition is ostensibly suppressed via the limitation on entry and on flock size, P.S. Ross' cost estimates are hardly authoritative either.

More importantly, the definition of what amounts to a "fair" return depends on which side of the transaction one looks. We are impressed, however, with Forbes' attempt, since his definition of "fair" return implies what capitalists generally expect to receive in investments elsewhere, the so-called "normal" or "competitive" return. While we agree that the Forbes/CAC accounting is far from unassailable, we are unwilling to join the producers, provincial egg boards, and CEMA officials in condemning it on the grounds it was conducted by "outsiders" to the industry.[45] If only those being regulated can do the regulating, the usual problem of social control emerges: *quis custodiet impos custodes?*

C. SECRET FEDERAL GOVERNMENT STUDY DM-10

In the Summer of 1976 the CAC secured for itself a "leaked" confidential Canadian federal government document, DM-10, on marketing boards, which purported to show that for 1975 egg prices were 9 cents per dozen "too high" for Canada in general.[46] We were unable to pursue this study's data base, but we are confident that the summary DM-10 is authentic.[47] It appears to be based on a comparison of Ontario egg prices with the U.S. Midwestern egg market prices. We will perform a similar exercise in the next part of this chapter, but we will concentrate on B.C. and her sister to the south, Washington State.

D. COMPARING THE PRICE OF FRESH EGGS IN B.C. AND WASHINGTON STATE

In the absence of CEMA, the BCEMB would be severely restricted in its ability to raise prices for fresh eggs much above the regional price. Since table eggs, because of their perishability, have a fairly limited geographic market, the price per dozen of B.C. fresh eggs in the absence of monopolistic restrictions could not—allowing transportation (3 to 4 cents) and tariff charges (3.5 cents)—deviate much more than 6 to 8 cents per dozen from Washington State prices.[48]

Further, and more important, even if trade in shell eggs between B.C. and Washington State were severely restricted by quotas, health restrictions, and other "hidden" tariffs, their respective prices under competitive conditions still could not diverge much. Their two major cost elements, feed grain and capital, have virtually identical prices on both sides of the border, whereas labour, which is $1 or more per hour higher in B.C., makes up only one-twentieth of the cost.[49] Land rental prices differ greatly (perhaps B.C.'s are 15 percent higher), but this element hardly makes up 10 percent of price. In all, even in the absence of trade in eggs, we would expect no more than a 5 to 7 cent difference in fresh egg prices between B.C. and Washington State, if B.C.'s market were competitive.

Table II-2 supports this contention, except for the pre-CEMA period, but not for the post-CEMA period (after 1973).[50] In fact, if we break up the data into two periods: 1960-1973, the pre-CEMA period, and 1973 until 1979, the post-CEMA period, we find that B.C. prices exceed Washington State's by some 4.1 cents (in 1975 prices) for the earlier period, but by 12.4 cents for the latter.[51] If only the supposedly free market period, i.e., the pre-BCEMB years (1961-67) are considered, the price difference becomes only 1.4 cents. For the period 1968 to 1972, the years when the B.C. Egg Board worked without CEMA's aid, this difference jumps to 9.1 cents. The post-CEMA data, which yield a 12.4 cent differential, are higher still. Imputing this latter

Table II-2

B.C. and Washington State
Fresh Egg Prices per Dozen

	(1)	(2)	(3)	(4)	(5)
Year	B.C. Price	Washington State Price	Washington State Price in Canadian $	Differences (1) minus (3)	(4) Adjusted for CPI (1975 prices)
1961	35.9	35.0	35.4	0.5	0.9
1962	35.4	32.6	34.9	0.5	0.9
1963	38.1	33.4	36.1	2.0	3.6
1964	32.1	31.9	34.4	−2.3	−4.0
1965	36.2	30.7	33.2	3.0	5.2
1966	38.5	36.9	39.8	−1.3	−2.2
1967	30.7	28.9	31.2	−0.5	−0.8
1968	37.1	29.7	32.1	5.0	7.7
1969	40.3	34.4	37.2	5.9	8.7
1970	37.9	32.6	33.9	4.0	5.6
1971	37.4	33.7	34.0	3.4	4.7
1972	40.8	26.7	26.4	14.4	19.0
1973	54.3	50.3	50.3	4.0	4.9
1974	66.5	47.0	46.1	20.4	22.6
1975	61.8	46.6	47.5	14.3	14.3
1976	67.1	54.1	53.6	13.5	12.6
1977	65.8	49.5	54.3	11.5	9.9
1978	66.6	47.3	53.9	12.7	10.0

Sources: Average of B.C. monthly prices, *Production of Eggs & Poultry*; average of Washington State monthly prices from U.S. Department of Agriculture, Statistical Reporting Services, *Washington Agricultural Prices*; exchange rates, *Bank of Canada Review*; Canadian Consumer Price Index from Statistics Canada series.

Note: Monthly prices are found by dividing the sales revenues by the volume of table eggs of all sizes. U.S. grading standards, while tolerating a greater weight variance per dozen, are similar to those in Canada: e.g., both types weigh about 25 ounces to the "Grade A large" dozen.

difference in price to CEMA and the BCEMB is an attractive hypothesis, since, as we said, it is otherwise most implausible, given the necessary similarities in overall cost structure between the two neighbouring units.

The fact that technical conditions of egg supply and factor prices in British Columbia are so similar, except for differences in land rental and labour prices, means real prices in B.C. and Washington should track very closely over time, except for changes in competitive conditions. Table II-3 provides statistics which attempt to test this. Fresh egg prices for each unit are divided by their respective consumer price indices and adjusted so that 1967, the year before the BCEMB came into being, equals 100 for both B.C. and Washington State. The ratios of these two indices indicate how real fresh egg prices in the two units moved relative to one another before and after the BCEMB. This last ratio indicates that before the BCEMB came into being B.C.'s real fresh egg price indices were, on average, almost identical to Washington's, but after that period the real price index for B.C. was 20 percent higher than in Washington.[52]

What is also interesting to notice is the movement of relative prices in each unit over time. In B.C., relative prices moved down slowly and erratically until 1968, when they shot back up, whereas in Washington State there was a decline over this first period that barely continued thereafter. This would indicate no discernible relative advantage of Washington State over B.C. eggs in the earlier (i.e., the pre-BCEMB, pre-CEMA) period, but a growing relative advantage in the post-egg board era. It is clear from this and the evidence on absolute differences in Table II-2 why there was growing pressure to keep out Washington eggs after the inception of CEMA.[53]

Of course, although we think it unlikely, other factors besides the BCEMB and CEMA could explain these price phenomena. In fact, in the next part of this chapter, we offer such powerful evidence of cartel behaviour that no doubt should remain in the reader's mind that higher than competitive returns have been earned as a result of the BCEMB's and the CEMA's joint supply management policies.

Table II-3

B.C. and Washington State Relative Fresh Egg Prices
(1967 = 1.00)

Year	(1) *Relative Price of B.C. Eggs*	(2) *Relative Price of Washington State Eggs*	(3) *Ratio of the Relative Price of B.C. to Washington State Eggs*
1961	1.35	1.35	1.00
1962	1.31	1.24	1.06
1963	1.39	1.26	1.10
1964	1.15	1.19	0.96
1965	1.26	1.12	1.13
1966	1.29	1.31	0.99
1967	1.00	1.00	1.00
1968	1.16	0.99	1.18
1969	1.21	1.08	1.12
1970	1.10	0.97	1.13
1971	1.05	0.96	1.09
1972	1.10	0.74	1.49
1973	1.36	1.31	1.03
1974	1.50	1.10	1.36
1975	1.26	1.00	1.25
1976	1.27	1.10	1.15
1977	1.15	0.94	1.22
1978	1.07	0.83	1.29

Sources: Average of B.C. monthly prices, *Production of Eggs & Poultry*; average of Washington State monthly prices from U.S. Department of Agriculture, Statistical Reporting Services, *Washington Agricultural Prices*; exchange rates, *Bank of Canada Review*; Canadian Consumer Price Index from Statistics Canada series.

Formulae: Col. 1 and Col. 2 = $(P_t^{eggs} \div P_{1967}^{eggs}) / (CPI_t \div CPI_{1967})$, but scaled so that 1967 = 1.00. Col. 3 = (1) $\div$ (2).

E. THE VALUE OF QUOTA

If the CEMA pricing formula yielded producers only a competitive return, the value of the legal right to produce a case of eggs (30 dozen per week, less some 15 percent adjustment)[54] would necessarily be zero. Put another way, *since the P.S. Ross report claims its pricing scheme yields only normal returns, one should find that quota rights have zero or negligible value. They do not.* But before we present this direct evidence of monopolistic practice, we must first explain on what basis quota prices are set and their relationship to noncompetitive returns.

First, let us consider the simplest and, for producers, ideal world of contrived supply. Here the egg board has monopoly power and uses it to maximize profits for the producer group. Monopoly rights in the form of quotas to supply eggs in particular quantities over specified times are distributed by the board to individual producers and are freely transferable among this latter group. Given that supply is restricted below the competitive level, each right to produce a case is worth a positive price. How much it is worth depends on the difference between the price at which eggs can be sold and their unit (average) cost of production for the marginal purchaser of the quota. This point requires some explanation and a graphical illustration, Figure 1, helps in this regard.

So long as rights to the monopoly quota Q_m are transferable, they will be allocated among producers such that industry cost is minimized. This must be the case or the maximum profit will not be realized, a condition logically not admissible if all producing parties are free to exchange. This implies, therefore, that the cost of production at the margins will be equal for all those who choose to retain quota or purchase same from those leaving the industry. (Renting quota is another possibility.) Further, since the price to be paid will be decided by the least efficient yet viable firm, the implicit rental price of quota per unit of Q will equal the difference between the price of the product, P_m, fetched by the output, Q_m, and the long-run supply, S_m.

Figure 1

The Fresh Egg Market with Restrictions
(Processed market ignored here)

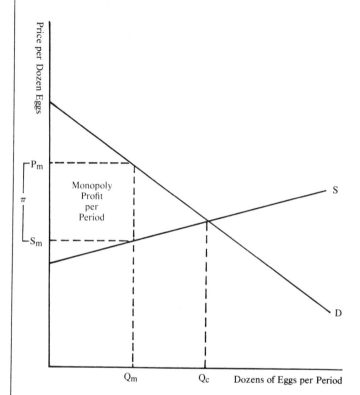

Explanation of Figure 1:
Q_c = the competitive output and Q_m = the restricted output. With output at Q_c, price just covers average opportunity cost for the marginal firm and the marginal opportunity cost for all firms. At the restricted output Q_m price exceeds the marginal opportunity cost by π.

The result of quota that restricts output below the competitive level is a gap between product (demand) price and the opportunity (supply) cost at the margins of producing another unit, π in Figure 1. The reader should note that this allocation is no different than if a tax of π cents per dozen were levied on eggs and its receipts distributed to those the government deemed worthy of public largesse. Alternatively, it is identical to a market where the government as the sole middleman puts bids out to purchase less than the competitive supply of fresh eggs for resale to consumers, and the resulting profit is distributed to those favoured by the policy.

Of course, if some restrictions on sale of quota among producers exist, as was the case in B.C. prior to 1976, the total value of quota rights would not be maximized, since industry costs would not be minimized. This will not mean lower prices for eggs—price is determined by consumers competitively bidding against one another for the available supply of eggs per period—but only lower prices for quota rights because of higher than necessary industry costs.[55]

It is unfortunate we do not know explicit rental prices of quota, because it would give us a direct measure of π, the monopoly mark-up. However, if we knew the trading prices of the full rights to the future use of quota, i.e., its present asset value, we could, with knowledge of its expected durability and the long-run producer interest rate used to discount the future stream, estimate π. This follows since quota value, V_π, can be written:

$$V_\pi = \pi_0 + \frac{\pi_1}{(1 + r)^1} + \ldots + \frac{\pi_n}{(1 + r)^n}$$

where the subscripts to π, 0 to n, refer to the period and r refers to the market discount rate. (We assume that π is unchanged over time in an expectational sense.)[56]

Luckily, some estimates of the present value of quota (in terms of 1975 dollars) are available. We have reason to believe that the present value of a quota right in 1972 was well in excess of $350 per case;[57] probably more than $550 in 1976, the first year quota was sold outright;[58] and at least

$750 and probably in excess of $1,000 in 1977.[59] (Forbes now claims that the price of quota is even higher, perhaps $1,300 for 1979, a figure we will not use, since it would only add upward bias to π.)[60] Doing a simple linear regression of these quota values yields an interpolated price of $550 to $800 (1975 dollars) for 1975.[61] Table II-4 gives estimates for three reasonable discount rates (8, 10, and 12 percent) and five lifespans for the monopoly returns (3, 5, 7, 10, and 15 years) respectively. These two ranges must surely bracket the plausible bounds for π.

We cannot "prove" that the plausible life of monopoly is 10 years or less, but given the growth of the consumers' movement and the threat, so far unsuccessful, of bringing marketing boards under the revised anti-combines legislation,[62] it would seem to make the contemplation of longer life

Table II-4

Value of the "Monopoly Mark-up," π, for 1975 Quota Value of $675/case[a]

(cents per dozen)

Expected Length of Quota's Life	Annual Discount Rates in %		
	8	*10*	*12*
3	19.0	19.6	20.2
5	12.3	12.9	13.5
7	9.4	10.1	10.7
10	7.4	8.0	8.7
15	5.8	6.5	7.3

Value of the monopoly mark-up, π, found by solving the equation:

$$\pi = \frac{V}{30} \sum \frac{r'}{1 + (1/(1-r')^t)}$$

where V is the quota value, r' is the weekly equivalent of the annual discount rates (i.e. an annual discount rate of .08 has a weekly equivalent of $1 - (1.08)^{1/52}$) and t is the number of weeks.

aThe average of the interpolated quota values for 1975. This is, in effect, the right to produce 85 percent of 30 dozen for 52 weeks. In calculating the table, therefore, $675/.85 has been used as the effective value of quota.

more imprudent. Likewise, three years seems too short if we mean a total cutoff of π in year 4. If we then take a 5 year life as the lower bound of expected life and 10 as the upper bound, it turns out that the mark-up per dozen eggs attributable to monopoly pricing is some 7 to 14 cents in excess of supply price or, again to take a central figure, some 11 cents.[63] This is very nearly in the mid-range of the Forbes/CAC study for Canada and almost that suggested in the government's Ontario focused DM-10 report.[64] It is about 4 cents less than Forbes' B.C. estimate.[65]

It is interesting to note here that, among others, Forbes and the CAC oppose the sale of quota between producers.[66] One must assume that they are against the sale of quota, on the theory that if a market price for them is not realized, neither is monopoly profit. Such an elementary confusion between a market determined residual, in this case profit, and opportunity cost restores our faith in the social productivity of professional economists. For, as we have shown above, quota value is the discounted value of current and future monopoly profits as determined in the market by the least efficient, but still viable, farm. If this market were suppressed we could be assured that trade in quota still would surface, but in other more costly ways, such as contracting out, cooperative actions of various sorts, and most definitely, merger.[67] Further, to the extent that such implicit and explicit merger is partially prohibited for reasons of policy or transactions cost, and scale economies are suppressed by not allowing trading in quota rights, we can confidently predict that unit costs to the marginal and many intramarginal producers will be above what they otherwise would be. The consequences of this will, among other things, dictate our discussion in the next chapter.

It should also be noted, at risk of didacticism, that it is an equally elementary proposition that, when avoidable cost to a wealth-maximizing monopolist rises, some of it is passed on to the consumer in higher prices. Since restrictions on quota transfers necessarily increase costs to the cartel, the predicted reaction is a further decrease in output.[68] Thus, no one obviously gains by prohibiting quota sales, but further losses to consumers are to be predicted. It may be, however, a necessary political measure to justify the aggregate output restrictions imposed, a point we shall explore in Chapters III and IV.

Chapter III
The Social Costs of Monopoly

All the different regulations of the mercantile system, necessarily derange more or less this natural and most advantageous distribution of the stock.

Smith, *Wealth of Nations*

It is not merely, or even mainly, that . . . [monopoly] *enables one set of people to mulct another set. It is that it causes resources to be held back from a form of investment in which the value of the marginal social product is greater than it is elsewhere.*

A.C. Pigou, *The Economics of Welfare*

Monopoly, besides, is a great enemy of good management, which can never be universally established but in consequence of the free and universal competition which forces everyone to have recourse to it for the sake of self defence.

Smith, *Wealth of Nations*

But there still remains, as an influence tending to produce [the seeking after monopoly privileges] *the direct expectations of the gains to which it may lead.*

Pigou, *The Economics of Welfare*

Monopolists must compete for monopoly status.
Alchian and Allen, *Exchange and Production*

To the man-on-the-street, the harm done by monopolistic restrictions can be expressed simply: the price of the product is too high. A slightly more sophisticated observer would tell us that the cost of monopoly is the excess of price charged over unit cost (including normal return to capital) multiplied by the activity's output per period. No doubt, the injustice of this matter will be vigorously asserted by both. Yet to the supplier of this good the transfer of income occasioned by this monopoly privilege will appear as simple "justice," especially since it is quite possible he or she bought the monopoly right from a previous owner.[69] Even if he or she is the original owner of the monopoly rights (or has through unanticipated higher returns already paid off the loan to purchase it), this producer will still more than likely view the continued transfer as morally justified. To paraphrase Ambrose Bierce's entry on tariffs in his *Devil's Dictionary*, monopoly is a useful device to protect producers from the greed of consumers.

If this were all there were to it—a philosophic argument over the just distribution of the surplus generated by a particular good's production and usage—the role of an economist in the discussion would be better served by the employment of a sensible moral philosopher or possibly even an applied theologian. Luckily for the well-being of economists, and hopefully for society, a great deal more useful analysis can be brought to the question of monopoly using economic theory.

In particular, economists have developed analytical devices which measure the cost of transferring income to producers via monopolistic restrictions. It is worthwhile, therefore, to spend some few paragraphs discussing how these measures are made.

First off, to an economist the word "cost" has a precise meaning: the value of what is given up by choosing one course of action rather than the next best. These opportunity costs can differ between individuals because of tastes or preferences, but more importantly because the costs of any action (and sometimes benefits) are not wholly borne by the chooser or, to use the economist's jargon, are not fully "internalized" by the decision maker. This means an individual may choose a course of action despite the fact that an alternative is socially superior (that is, the true opportunity costs of the former are greater than the realized gains), because he or she does not bear the entire burden of the rejected alternative.

In a world where decision-making efforts come free, it is obvious that all social costs would be private costs, that is, fully internalized; hence, there could be no divergence between the interests of any two or more persons overlooked in an exchange, no matter how complex the social relationship. For example, it is well-known (and we shall demonstrate) that the gain to producers of restricting competitive outcomes is exceeded by the losses imposed on consumers. This gain foregone by preventing competition involves a social cost not borne by the suppliers. If transactions were costless, however, consumers could "bribe" producers to increase output, and both groups would be made better off. Put differently, starting at a monopoly position, consumers would gain more by a movement to a competitive outcome than producers would lose. Since all of us are consumers as well as producers, it is reasonable to argue that on the whole we would all gain by an economic compact or social contract which prohibited monopolistic practices.[70]

Unfortunately, the world we live in is one where the cost of transacting such efficient Roussovian social contracts is excessively high. Economic policy analysis, therefore, is an aid to the politicians' decisions on how the property rights of consumers and producers should be allocated, if wealth is to be jointly maximized.[71] In this section of our studies, measures, *meant to be taken more as orders of magnitude than exact figures*, are offered of what the citizens of British Columbia lose because of the existence of a noncompetitive market in fresh eggs. Against this loss these same citizens and their agents, public officials, can then consider the efficacy of other methods of transferring income to those currently holding monopoly rights (quota), or they can even consider their confiscation, that is, their noncompensated expropriation. In this sense our measure is a social cost estimate to enhance the decision makers' (and in turn their constituents') abilities to choose with care. In a larger sense, however, it suggests that the magnitude of damage in this market—as one of many similar distortions in a multitude of market situations—is sufficiently large that some thought should be given to the disutility of noncompetitive restrictions in general. No accurate measure of this larger loss to the Province of British Columbia or Canada is, or even probably can be, made. Nonetheless, we can say with some confidence that the losses in the large sense are not negligible.[72]

Naturally, if other social benefits of a noncompetitive market exist, they should be weighed against the economic costs. In other words, the numbers that emerge in Chapter III should be viewed as rough measurements to aid the decision maker, a public "price tag" if you will, not as proof of the undesirability of this particular monopoly.[73]

Having asserted that the social costs of monopoly exceed the gains to those possessing these rights, it is necessary, if tedious, to explain on what conceptual grounds these cost-benefit calculations are made. This requires a short review of the elementary theory of demand and supply that some readers will recall (happily, we hope) from their elementary economics course.

A. A NOTION OF A COMPETITIVE OPTIMAL ALLOCATION

Supply curves represent the quantity of offerings made by individual firms at various prices. As a price rises so, too, does the quantity of the commodity or service offered by the supplying firms. Economists confidently assert that this decision to supply is a self-interested one, which means that at any point on this curve the price reflects the private costs of the alternatives foregone in realizing that increment of output. More specifically, each profitseeking firm will choose an output that equates the extra (or marginal) cost of securing that increment in quantity with the increase in realized returns. Since in a competitive (price-taking) setting the gross return is measured by firms in terms of the market price, the supply curve is said to represent at each point the marginal cost to society of producing this output.[74] Thus, in Figure 2, the area under the supply curve for the competitive output, the trapezoid $OQ_cB\alpha$, measures the total value of the resources used to produce the competitive output Q_c, where supply (given by the schedule αS) equals demand (schedule βD), and the marginal cost equals market price (P_c).

The demand curve has a similar economic interpretation. Consumers are considered competent to judge the value of the commodity and weigh its value against price charged.[75] To maximize their own welfare, consumers' self-interest drives them to purchase commodities up to the point where the satisfaction measured in dollars from an additional unit is just equal to the extra cost, the price charged.[76]

Since the price at which consumers are willing to purchase each quantity of output is given by the demand curve, the latter can then be interpreted as the consumers' preference maximizing value of the marginal unit at each output. In Figure 2, the marginal value consumers place on Q_c is P_c, but at Q_m it rises to P_m, reflecting the "law of demand." The total value consumers place on consuming the product is given by the area under B D for the chosen output, which, for competition, is $OQ_cB\beta$.

Thus, consumers value the competitive output by the area $OQ_cB\beta$, while producers would be willing to offer it for anything more than the area $OQ_cB\alpha$. Therefore, the net gain to society when Q_c is produced and purchased at P_c is the triangular area $\alpha B\beta$. This gain is split between consumers and producers in the amounts given by triangles βP_cB and αP_cB, respectively. The first triangle, the difference between what consumers would willingly pay rather than do without the product and what they are required to pay by the market, is called *consumers' surplus* or *consumers' rent*. The second triangle, the difference between what producers actually receive from the market and what they (explicitly or implicitly) pay factors whose cooperation produced that output, is termed *producers' surplus* or *producers' rent*.[77]

Figure 2

Simple Supply-Demand Measures of Joint Rents to Consumers and Producers

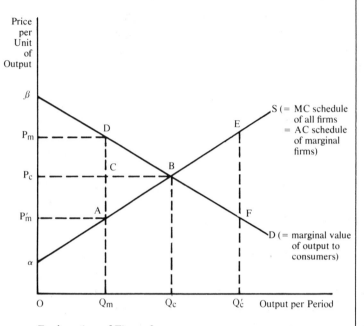

Explanation of Figure 2:

At Q_c Consumers' gain is $\beta P_c B$
   Producers' gain is $\alpha P_c B$
   Total gain is $\alpha B \beta$
At Q_m Consumers' gain is $\beta P_m D$
   Producers' gain is $\alpha P_m DA$
   Total gain is $\alpha \beta DA$
Net loss of moving from Q_c to Q_m is ABD.

B. THE SOCIAL COSTS OF DEVIATIONS FROM THE COMPETITIVE NORM

What should be clear from construction of Figure 2 is that any output other than Q_c will not maximize the joint surplus or rents of producers and consumers. If, for example, output was expanded from Q_c to Q_c' because of a subsidy, opportunity costs would exceed consumer benefits for the $Q_c Q_c'$ units by triangle BFE. Economists then would say that the social cost of the subsidized output is area BFE, by which they mean the net loss of welfare in choosing Q_c' over the competitive output Q_c.

In the case of eggs it was demonstrated in Chapter II that the BCEMB and CEMA successfully created monopoly rights for select producers, and this caused the supply of fresh eggs to contract below the competitive level. Since the price of fresh eggs necessarily rose as a result, consumers' surplus fell by less than producers' rents increased; in other words, the net loss is triangle ABD, as previously discussed. We shall measure this in the next section.

The reader is forewarned, however, that this particular loss is usually trivial, and the findings of this study are no exception.[78] Three other more serious deviations from competitive behaviour, however, will concern us in analyzing the social cost of the BCEMB. The first is caused by regulatory impediments causing productive efficiency to be limited by severely restricting input and output choices by individual egg farmers. The second is caused by excessive production and diversion to the breaker market of fresh quality eggs. The last is caused by the lure and protection of the monopoly profit itself or as economists call it, "rent-seeking" actions. Each of these, and the traditional "triangle" cost, will be discussed in the next four parts of this section.

C. MEASURING THE TRADITIONAL "DEADWEIGHT" LOSS OF MONOPOLY FOR THE B.C. EGG MARKETING SCHEME

The triangle ABD in Figure 2 is the traditional measure of monopoly damage. As stated above, it is the cost of restricting output in the market below the competitive level.

The area of this triangle can be approximated by the formula:

$$W_T = \frac{1}{2} \cdot \left(\frac{\eta}{\eta/\sigma' - 1}\right) \left(\frac{\pi}{P_m}\right)^2 \cdot E$$

where η is the demand price elasticity; σ' is the product of the supply price elasticity and the ratio of the monopoly price at Q_m to the supply price (P_m/P_m'); π, the monopoly mark-up, is the difference $(P_m - P_m')$, and E, sales volume, is the product of P_m and Q_m.[79]

$(P_m - P_m')$ (for 1975, to conform with the Forbes/CAC findings, as well as with the other corroborations mentioned in the last section) is 11 cents. The actual annual marketing quota was 31,000 cases per week (Table I-2) or 48.4 million dozens for the year. P_m was 62 cents (Table II-2).

The price elasticity of demand for eggs varies between -0.25 and -1.50.[80] We shall use -0.75 as a reasonable, if actually conservative, measure biasing W_T downward.

The supply elasticity offered by R.M.A. Loyns and W.F. Lu for Canada of $+1.0$ seems too low to us. Our argument is simple. With labour and land being a trivial portion of costs, and with capital, laying hens, and feed mash virtually in perfect elastic supply, only "expertise" can be the scarce, supply price raising factor. Discussions with those in the industry in academic positions, government, and business convinces us that "expertise" is in highly elastic supply. Therefore, σ is probably not different from $+\infty$, but, again to add to the conservatism of our estimate, we will assume $\sigma = +5.0$.[81]

With σ of $+5.0$, W_T is $308,000 (and climbs only to $350,000 when $\sigma = \infty$). Furthermore, price would fall by almost 10 cents if (a) the egg board made quota freely available to all existing and potential entrants, but (b) the 1975 restriction of 200 cases per farm was enforced. (If $\sigma = \infty$, price would fall the full 11 cents.) Output would rise by almost 12 percent to 53.8 million dozens per year (and only by 13 percent to 53.9 million dozens in 1975 if $\sigma = \infty$).

To put it differently, consumers currently transfer 11

cents per dozen directly to producers—almost $5.3 million per year. Indirectly, because of substitution, additional losses of consumer surplus (the triangle DCB in Figure 2) of another $275,000 are given up to inefficiency. Producers gain the $5.3 million per year transfer but in the process lose producer surplus (triangle ABC in Figure 2) equal to $32,000 for 1975. In other words, at a cost of over $7 per household for 1975,[82] $23,000 was effectively transferred to each producer. As a percentage of the net transfer, society wasted around 6 percent of the resources involved in the transfer, or 1 percent as a percentage of actual farm gate sales.

D. THE REGULATORY COSTS OF THE B.C. EGG BOARD

Because farms cannot currently (and legally) exceed weekly quotas of approximately 300 cases (except for those "grandfathered" by having larger operational sizes when the BCEMB came into existence), important economies of scale are lost in the process.

A comparison of B.C. and Washington State farms, Table III-1, is instructive here. Washington State has no restriction on either entry or size of firms, hence competitive market forces determine the size distribution of farms. The reader will note in Washington that (a) farms are much larger

Table III-1
Farm Size, Washington State and B.C., January 1975

Flock Size (Birds)	Percent of Producers		Percent of Output	
	Washington	*B.C.*	*Washington*	*B.C.*
up to 10,000	24.7	57.7	2.9	29.3
10,000 to 50,000	64.3	41.7	31.7	65.8
over 50,000	21.0	0.7	65.4	4.9

Sources: Washington State figures from unpublished data provided by Daniel K. Andrews, Extension Poultry Scientist, Western Washington Research and Extension Center, Puyallup, Washington (1976). B.C. data from *Annual Report* of the BCEMB (April 1976).

in terms of flock size and (b) the larger farms dominate the market in terms of share of output. This means it is likely that important scale economies are foregone in B.C. as a result of BCEMB limitation.[83] One crude notion of this 300-quota right limitation cost can be gleaned from the first CEMA study by P.S. Ross.[84] The P.S. Ross cost per dozen estimates at the farm gate are shown in Table III-2.

Table III-2

Egg Production Cost in Canada

Flock Size (Birds)	Current Required Quota (Cases)[a]	Cents/Dozen
up to 12,000	up to 169	51.5
12,000 to 24,000	169 to 338	54.8
24,000 to 48,000	338 to 676	56.0
48,000 and up	over 676	47.8

Sources: P.S. Ross, "An Examination of Egg Production Costs in Canada: A report to the Canadian Egg Marketing Agency." Flock sizes are converted in terms of quota by the BCEMB ratio of 71 birds per case.

[a]Based on the current regulation that a farm have only 71 laying birds (over 20 months of age) for every case of quota.

The careful reader will immediately note that in the last chapter we argued that the P.S. Ross data was not wholly persuasive, at least not to Forbes and his CAC colleagues. A careful reading of Forbes *et al.*, however, suggests that they do not disagree with the findings as to unit cost differences between sizes of farms, but only to their absolute levels.[85] Thus, it is simple, given Tables III-1 and III-2, to calculate the change in average cost that would accompany freeing up the sale of quota between producers. If output limitations on individual firms were relaxed, the competitive output, Q_c (fresh and breaker) eggs would have been produced according to the size distribution that reflected overall industry cost minimization, not constrained, as we assumed in the last part of this section of our study.[86] Assuming that the distribution of firm sizes that would emerge is not too far different from Washington State's (Table III-2), the average cost (P.S. Ross figures) would fall from 54.9 cents to 50.3 cents or by 3.6 cents.[87] Thus producer cost savings would be $1.8 million per year.[88] We shall label this W_{R1}. (Graphically, we show this as trapezoid $\kappa J A \alpha$ in Figure 3.)

This significant loss requires some explanation. Why would the BCEMB prohibit unlimited sales of quota rights and mergers between producers if so much is to be gained (an annual average of $8,000 per producer)?

We think the answer becomes clear if one asks the question, how many firms would the industry contain if the size distribution were permitted to evolve toward efficient sizes? If the total output were spread across firms, as in Washington State, where incentives and legal rights to economic rationalization exist, the numbers of firms would decline from (the 1975 number of) 227 to no more than 70.[89] Such a huge reduction in their numbers would mean that on average each firm would have to hold at least 500 units of quota and would perforce have to have had a capitalized value on quota alone of over $500,000 in 1975 dollars. The argument of maintaining the family farm put by BCEMB and CEMA could hardly be sustained when the average egg farm is three to four times its current size. Further, such a dramatic diminishing of their numbers might well decrease their effective political weight. Thus, the $1.8 million lost in 1975 because of unexhausted scale economies may be a wise political investment on the part of the industry.

John McManus has offered us an important addendum to this argument. He points out that the *raison d'être* given the public for the existence of CEMA and its provincial membership is the plight of the small family farm. Furthermore, the practical mechanism used to set price, the so-called cost-of-production formula, is based upon costs to this entity. A rationalized industry structure with firms three to four times larger than the current size would make such a formula difficult to defend.[90]

Further, since we know that the large farms with huge

Figure 3
Welfare Costs of Production Inefficiencies of Egg Board

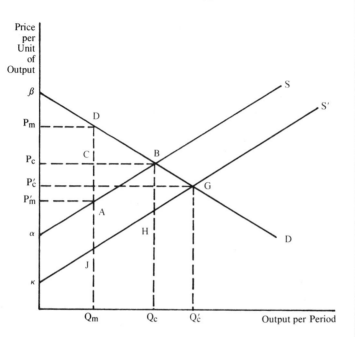

Explanation of Figure 3:

At Q_m productive inefficiency alone costs producer W_{R1}. At Q'_c the social gains to productive efficiency, i.e., absenting W_T, is $W_R = W_{R1}$ (parallelogram $\kappa JA\alpha$) + W_{R2} (parallelogram JHBA) + W_{R3} (triangle HGB). Consumers gain trapezoid P'_cGBP_c; therefore producers' welfare change is $W_R - P'_cGBP_c$.

"grandfathered" quotas have a great stake in maintaining the small-farm pricing formula, we can predict they will lobby for its continuance, plus the severe attenuation of rights to transfer quota that it implies. We also know, however, that over time the BCEMB has permitted the average size of farms to rise slowly, so this "grandfathered" group does not wholly dominate the margins of the board's choice. Small holders would gain by permitting transfers as scale economies are realized, but would lose, as we conjectured earlier, if these savings were to jeopardize the "family-farm" pricing formula employed. On net, therefore, the latter group's pressure on the BCEMB to allow free transfer is predictably much less than would otherwise be the case.

The question of scale economies and losses to producers under BCEMB restrictions (W_{R1} of Figure 3) is, while interesting, only part of social cost. The reader will recall that what we are attempting to measure is what (in part, at least) is lost by not permitting a competitive organization of the industry. What is required is not just a measure of W_{R1}, but of W_{R2} and W_{R3} in Figure 3. This follows since competition, along with a deregulation of firm sizes, would lead to a downward shift in the supply function from S to S'. This indicates that more output can be produced at a given set of prices because of superior internal organization of the industry.

For a measure of W_{R2} = JHBA and W_{R3} = HGB, however, we must be conjectural in our estimates. We will assume that S shifts down to S', more or less in a parallel fashion, by two-thirds the amount of the per unit cost savings (3.5 cents) at Q_m. We realize that it is arbitrary to assume that this downward shift equals 2.5 cents, but the assumption recognizes that changes in industry marginal cost will be less than in the average cost, since some of the existing firms are already near or above the scale at which per unit cost economies are exhausted.

Since we know Q_m from the data (48.4 million dozens) and Q_c by previous hypothesis (53.8 million dozens), assuming the downshift as 2.5 cents (and constant over the relevant range) allows us to estimate W_{R2} as \$148,000. Measuring W_{R3} can be accomplished using an amended formula for W_T:

$$W_{R3} = \frac{1}{2} \cdot \left(\frac{\eta}{\eta/\sigma'' - 1}\right) \left(\frac{\delta}{P_c}\right)^2 \cdot E'$$

where σ'' is the supply price elasticity multiplied by the ratio P_c to $(P_c - \delta)$, and E' is the product of P_c and Q_c, where δ is the downshift of S to S' in Figure 3. Recalling our estimate of $P_c = 52$ cents, $Q_c = 53.8$ million, $\sigma = +5.0$, and our "guesstimate" of δ as 2.5 cents, W_{R3} emerges as \$21,000, a number so trivial as to invite our conscious oversight. Price would fall to 50 cents and output would expand some 0.6 million dozens to 54.4 million dozens.[91]

Looking at Figure 3 again, the whole area given by the sum $W_R = W_{R1} + W_{R2} + W_{R3}$ can be estimated as about \$2 million for 1975. It is useful here to ask just how this \$2 million efficiency gain on the production side would be split between producers and consumers.

Recall that the realization of scale economies causes S to shift to S'. As a result, P_c falls to P_c' and output rises from Q_c to Q_c'. Consumers gain from this the dollar equivalent of the trapezoid $P_c' G B P_c$. This is the sum of the rectangle with height $(P_c - P_c')$, and length Q_c, plus the triangle of length $(Q_c' - Q_c)$, also of height $(P_c - P_c')$. The difference between P_c and P_c' was taken to be 2.5 cents and the quantities $Q_c = 53.8$ and $Q_c' = 54.4$ million dozens respectively. The arithmetic yields about a \$1 million total for consumer gains to production efficiency alone, given competitive pricing. Since $W_R = $ \$2 million, this means that producers would gain \$1 million or half the total of W_R.

Putting it all together, $W_T + W_R$, an end to the BCEMB/CEMA control would, on the basis only of the costs noted, improve consumers welfare by \$6 million per year, or almost \$9 per household, while producers would lose \$3.9 million, or some \$18,000 per farm, annually.

Given the well-known difficulty of organizing consumer interest, because of the microscopically lower per household returns and their large numbers *vs.* the much lower organization cost and dramatically higher per firm stakes of getting producers together, it should be clear why Mark Twain's "theorem" generally holds; to wit: the free traders win the debates, but the protectionists always get the votes.[92]

E. OTHER REGULATORY COSTS

Besides the costs imposed by restricting expansion of egg farms to their optimal size, two other impediments to efficient operation exist that would be absent under a competitive framework. The first involves excessive diversion of fresh eggs to the breaker market, and the other is one of quality control.

We have so far taken only casual notice of the breaker market. In the production of eggs, however, regardless of the attention lavished on a flock's health and feed, and the care exercised in collection, a certain percentage of eggs are likely to become "seconds" or "cracks." Furthermore, because of the variable nature of demand and supply and intense consumer preference for freshness, Grade A or B eggs are often downgraded to Grade C or cracks for reason of excessive shelf life.

This means the supply of both kinds of eggs, shell and breaker, can usefully be thought of as occurring in relatively fixed proportions. Historically in Canada, before marketing boards, this ratio was about 4 to 96 but since CEMA it has risen to 7 to 93, according to the Food Prices Review Board.[93] Table III-3 corroborates this. From 1960 through 1967, the period before provincial egg boards, an average of 3.7 percent of total domestic egg production went to the processed market. In the period 1967 through 1972, when every province save Newfoundland had an egg board (Newfoundland is excluded in Table III-3), this percentage rose to 4.9 percent. Since 1973 this figure has averaged slightly in excess of 7 percent.

CEMA's *Annual Reports* have acknowledged the difficulty of maintaining production within quota. Setting prices in excess of production cost meant that farmers had incen-

Table III-3

Canadian Egg Production, 1960-1977
(Newfoundland excluded)

Year	% Broken[a]	% Exported	% Imported
1960	3.6	2.5	0.4
1961	3.0	1.5	1.1
1962	3.7	0.3	0.9
1963	3.2	0.4	2.1
1964	4.1	0.5	0.5
1965	3.4	0.2	1.4
1966	3.4	0.3	4.2
1967	5.2	0.2	4.5
1968	4.1	0.2	2.9
1969	3.7	0.5	3.0
1970	5.4	1.4	2.5
1971	5.8	0.7	0.8
1972	5.3	0.4	1.2
1973	5.7	2.6	0.9
1974	7.3	3.1	1.8
1975	6.5	2.4	2.7
1976	6.8	0.6	2.8
1977[b]	9.3	2.4	0.8

Source: Poultry Division and Markets Information Branch, Department of Agriculture, *Poultry Market Review*.

[a]Based on registered plant production only.
[b]Based on September figures.

tive to produce in excess of their allowable quota. (In 1977 bird counts were introduced to aid in enforcement.) The result has been an "excess" of eggs coming into the market. Price in the fresh market could only be maintained by diverting acceptable shell eggs to the breaker market. In all probability, some others were also downgraded and shipped abroad, mostly to the U.S.[94] Evidence for the latter is also shown on Table III-3. Between 1960 and 1967, Canada exported 0.7 percent and about the same percentage from 1968 to 1972, but in the post-CEMA period this percentage tripled to 3.3 percent. Of course, this might have been offset by imports (again see Table III-3), but logic would not support this, because the federal government in 1974 and 1975 imposed temporary import restrictions and formalized them on July 4, 1975.[95] The government admitted the reason was to strengthen its ability to control domestic supply, a position they later defended on the basis of Article XI of the General Agreement on Tariffs and Trade (GATT).[96] This immediately provoked a stream of objections from the American Farm Bureau, the United Egg Producers, and several prominent American politicians.[97] Now, given the highly elastic world demand for processed eggs,[98] it is wholly unlikely this storm of protest could have involved anything but a restriction on U.S. exports of shell eggs.

What this means is that it is reasonable to treat the Canadian market as diverting at least 7 percent and perhaps as high as 9 percent of egg production to the breaker and downgraded markets within Canada and abroad. Since historically only 4 percent were so directed, it would seem reasonable to assert that about 3 percent of the total production of fresh eggs have been "dumped" at prices below their production cost. Since B.C. production cost is about 51 cents and, according to both Forbes and McManus, cracks were around 30 cents during this period, with total output of 48.4 million dozens, losses borne by levies on producers would be over $300,000, if diversions of fresh eggs by surplus removals in B.C. followed the overall Canadian pattern.[99] This is a total loss; because of the worldwide nature of the processed market, it is not possible to lower breaker prices to any significant extent, especially over the long run. A suggestion exists, however, that like the traditional measure, W_T, this loss is a small part of the inefficiency burden occasioned by the egg board.[100] And well it should be, if economics is to be any guide. As McManus has shown for broilers, marketing boards probably will attempt to reduce inefficiencies to a minimum, when the burdens of the inefficiencies are borne chiefly by their members.[101]

The other regulatory issue we now wish to take up involves quality deterioration.[102] As the reader undoubtedly knows, eggs are graded by weight and quality. Such words as "Grade A Large" are not, however, sufficient to assure the purchaser of quality in its more subtle dimensions. In the absence of marketing boards, wholesale purchasers of eggs (graders, wholesalers, and some large retailers) had unique personal and ongoing relationships with producers. Further, both buyers and sellers of this commodity are able to ascertain the quality of such subtle attributes as age, colour and firmness of yolk, ratio of yolk to white, and so on, that we generally think of when we speak of "freshness" and "quality." It turns out, however, that no low cost grading mechanism can accurately ascertain these less visible dimensions of the product. It is known, nevertheless, that correlations exist between these desirable but ungradeable attributes and objective traits such as mash quality (positive) and age of hen (positive over the early laying life and negative later). Because consumers have choice among retail purchasers and can detect quality differences, pre-BCEMB graders and wholesalers had the incentive to contract among producers, tailoring price offers according to expected quality. The continuous nature of these dealings, plus the ease by which intermediate buyers could monitor crucial, quality related inputs of egg production, ensured that chiseling on these expectations was not serious.

The advent of marketing boards severed, in part at least, these direct relationships between egg farmers and their intermediate purchasers. The need to monitor quota rules meant that farmers could no longer deal directly with these middlemen and large retailers, since neither intermediate buyers nor individual producers had any incentive to police quota.[103] The BCEMB required, therefore, that sales be made to the Board's official grading stations. Since the latter have not the same incentive to monitor the "invisibles," and since it costs farmers more to produce higher rather than lower quality eggs, the predicted result is some falling off in average quality. This will be mitigated by farmers' collective desire to maintain the reputation of B.C. eggs, but only in a crude sense, since it is well-known that agents of collective nonprofit groups have less incentives than their counterparts in profit oriented firms to carry out the necessary and costly monitoring processes.[104] Therefore, farmers' collective demand to police themselves will be only partially supplied by the BCEMB's grading agents.

Unfortunately, little other than anecdotal evidence, and no statistical measure of the magnitude of this quality deterioration, can be given for B.C. or Canada, in general. Whetstone, however, did find one piece of evidence in the U.K. which confirms this prediction.[105] Prior to the dissolution of the British Egg Marketing Board (hereafter BEMB), all eggs receiving the public subsidy were bought and resold by the BEMB. Consumers could readily recognize this, too, because the logo of the BEMB was placed on all subsidized eggs. Nonsubsidized eggs could be sold, however, but at a higher nonsubsidized price (some 10 or more additional cents per dozen in 1975 terms). Whetstone noted that these higher priced, non-BEMB eggs were sold in noteworthy quantities. She argued it was the higher perceived quality, namely "freshness," that explained this premium.

For Figures 2 and 3 this means that the observed demand curve for eggs lies slightly below that which would otherwise be obtained if the BCEMB was not in existence. The area above the new price line and between these curves, less the area between the new and old price lines bounded by the old demand curve, would measure this quality deterioration loss.[106] Of course, higher quality means increased production cost, so supply costs would shift up too. Because of lack of hard data, however, we are unable to measure quality loss and impute a dollar loss. Our casual empiricism based on unscientific samplings of eggs purchased in Washington State and the Lower Mainland of B.C. suggests this loss is negligible, especially compared to the losses suffered from the nonexploitation of scale economies. At this point we shall assume that it is zero, but further research is in order.[107]

F. THE ORGANIZATIONAL COSTS OF MONOPOLIZING

Two hundred years ago, in his *Wealth of Nations*, Adam Smith noted that monopolies (for reasons other than scale economies or informational scarcities) are usually creatures of the state. This remains true today. Furthermore, monopolies are not distributed randomly, as Stigler notes,[108] but are found in particular sectors of Western economies—agriculture, transportation, finance, and public utilities, but not in clothing, retail sales, nonprofessional services, and manufacturing. Such a pattern seems hardly a random effect of collective choice.

How, why, and where regulatory monopolies arise is a most interesting question, but it unfortunately requires a great deal of discussion for adequate consideration of the issues.[109] Suffice it to say for our purposes that monopoly privileges are demanded and supplied in quantities and at prices depending on the legal constraints of society (common law, statutes, and constitutional law which determine the distribution of political assets in the community) and on the relative costs of both organizing and blocking monopoly seeking coalitions. What a group is willing to pay for these privileges, the demand price, reflects the net gains monopolists receive over what they would realize under a competitive regime. What is actually paid is also a function of supply, the costs politicians bear in providing these rights, with due allowance for misinformation, error, and the market in political entrepreneurship. Unfortunately, although economists know why private groups lobby and try to attract political entrepreneurs to get monopolies, they are unsure why the wishes of certain private interests are so readily fulfilled. No doubt, it has to do with the costliness of organizing such diverse groups as consumers, compared with more compact ones, like producers.[110]

Ippolito and Masson found in their study of the U.S. milk program[111] that the cost of achieving monopoly profits due to political and other "rent seeking" activity on behalf of producers was more than trivial. They estimated that one-fourth of the annual rent created as a result of the program was dissipated in various costs of lobbying to support the higher than competitive price of milk.[112] If this were true for eggs as well, and we have only sketchy evidence that it is, this would turn out to be a waste of almost $1.0 million for 1975, or around 2 cents per dozen, since, as we have shown, producers would forego almost $4 million if the provincial and national egg boards were disbanded ($5 million of transfers less $1.3 million to be saved from realized scale economies and no excessive surplus removals). Forbes has noted for 1977 that almost 40 percent of levies go to the BCEMB's and CEMA's administration. Some of this, 3 percent, is spent on advertising, a legitimate activity of a free market organization, although this still amounts to ten times the spending in the U.S. by the United Egg Producers and the American Egg Board.[113] Assuming that 35 percent of levies are for policing and enforcing quota rules and for lobbying activity, the cost per dozen for organizational maintenance is almost 1.5 cents per dozen, or almost $0.7 million for 1975, close to Ippolito's and Masson's finding.[114]

G. SUMMATION OF SOCIAL COSTS

We have in this third chapter attempted to explain how economists measure monopoly damages and then used these concepts to get a notion of what the social loss from the BCEMB actually is. This net loss to society of the BCEMB and CEMA is about $3.3 million per year, or 11 percent of the gross annual farm gate value of table eggs.[115] Thus, to hypothesize that almost one-eighth of the gross value to farmers of B.C. eggs is lost because of all the forementioned restrictions is probably not too far off the mark. This is no different in effect from slightly more than one egg in each dozen of eggs produced in B.C. being deliberately broken by state fiat, a situation that, surely, would upset all parties to the market and their representatives. Table III-4 summarizes our estimates based on these discussions.

Because, however, these costs are borne by consumers whose per family stakes in reform are tiny (less than $10 per

Table III-4

Annual Gains and Losses
Attributed to the BCEMB/CEMA
(1975 estimates and prices)

Consumers	*Losses* *($000,000s)*
Direct transfers to producers	5.3
Deadweight triangle	0.3
Quality deterioration	probably negligible
Additional losses due to foregone scale economies	1.0
Total losses	*6.6*
[Per household losses almost $10]	

Producers	*Gains* *($000,000s)*	*Losses* *($000,000s)*
Direct transfers from consumers	5.3	
Deadweight triangle	negligible	
Foregone scale economies		1.0
Excess surplus removals		0.3
Maintaining board as monitor and lobbyist		0.7
Total net gain	*3.3*	
[Per farm net gain $14,500]		

Aggregate Social Costs	
Total net losses	$3,300,000
Net losses per household	almost $5
Net social cost per farm	$14,500
Losses as percent of farm gate sales	11%
Consumer losses as percent of net transfer received by producers	50%

Note: This table is a summary of the discussion in Chapter II. See the earlier parts of the text for relevant caveats.

year), and because the $5.0 million annual monopoly profit (less $2.00 million in competitive rents lost due to inefficiencies and cartel maintenance costs) to producers leads to a tremendously high per farm gain (a net of almost $14,000 per farm), we are somewhat doubtful that anything will be done about this cartel *taken in isolation*. Nevertheless, when the sum of all marketing board damages is considered, and the gains from other regulatory reform are contemplated, the gain to political entrepreneurship of consumer defence rises. As the late and distinguished Canadian economist, Harry G. Johnson, often pointed out, the sum of many small magnitudes is likely to be large.[116] That many elected officials, spurred on by public interest groups, sense the political profit of removing monopoly privileges is an interesting idea to follow.[117]

H.   REMARKS ON OFFSETTING GAINS

Before closing we would like to note an argument made in favour of the BCEMB and its federal ally, CEMA, on the basis of risk reduction. Consumers and producers, argue these boards, gain when the variance in price around the mean is reduced, since they all dislike risk. Table III-5 compares the coefficients of variation between B.C. and Washington State over time.[118] This suggests that marketing boards have reduced the relative dispersion of price.[119]

The benefits of such price stability to producers will be reflected in quota values, since they will lower the costs of doing business. As such, we have not really taken this benefit into account in Table III-4, since, under competition, risk costs would rise. To the extent they do rise, consumers will pay higher prices. But as we have seen, consumers have not received lower prices. In fact, if the monthly data of Table III-5 are compared, with due allowance for exchange rate and price level differences (to ensure rough comparability), one can see that in general the peaks of Washington State prices exceed the troughs. The "insurance policy" offered B.C. consumers is one where the premium exceeds the contemplated losses.

Table III-5

Relative Monthly Price Variation in British Columbia and Washington State (coefficient of variation)

	British Columbia	*Washington State*
1964	9.2	5.6
1965	11.3	11.6
1966	8.5	11.5
1967	10.0	14.5
1968	14.5	12.8
1969	8.3	17.2
1970	7.7	22.3
1971	4.3	24.2
1972	3.3	15.6
1973	10.1	16.2
1974	6.3	17.7
1975	4.9	13.5
1976	1.9	8.8
1977	3.9	9.4
1978	2.8	8.8
1979	3.4	n.a.

Sources: Average of B.C. monthly prices, *Production of Eggs and Poultry*; average of Washington State monthly prices from U.S. Department of Agriculture, Statistical Reporting Services, *Washington Agricultural Prices*; exchange rates, *Bank of Canada Review*; Canadian Consumer Price Index from Statistics Canada Series.

We ought to mention further that price variability in itself is not very costly, if such variability is correctly anticipated. If movements in product and input prices are correctly anticipated, there is no risk. One way this could be encouraged is by the creation by Agriculture Canada of a forward market such as the Chicago Mercantile Exchange which, through "futures contracts," allows egg farmers to hedge with up to six month contracts. We do not necessarily recommend this be done with public funds, however, without some serious research on the subject. What gives us pause here is the knowledge that such structured, futures markets for eggs did not exist in pre-egg board Canada. This could have been because of "thinness" in the scope of the market or from lack of interest on the part of buyers and sellers. Neither would positively support the social utility of government subsidy of a forward market mechanism except, perhaps, when the current, wasteful alternatives are concerned.[120]

Three other claims for marketing boards bear comment here as well. First, it is said, they preserve the "family farm." Second, and related, they encourage small business in what would otherwise be a controlled noncompetitive agro-business. Third, without marketing boards it is unlikely that farmers could earn competitive incomes.

We readily admit that the BCEMB probably has fought the trend toward larger egg farms, but we remind the reader that this has meant a waste of productive resources in lost scale economies of $1 million for 1975. The Jeffersonian notion of an independent and populous yeomanry was an eighteenth- and early nineteenth-century reaction to the political power of landed gentry—a British, not North American, phenomenon. We do not see what political costs Canadian society (as opposed to representatives of rural ridings) will bear if the reduction of the labour to land ratio, already a dramatic fact in agriculture, is allowed to continue.[121] We would like to see some objective, operational argument be given for the maintenance of rural populations at levels beyond those that would obtain with individuals seeking out their own best use of their own resources.

We also admit that without marketing boards like the BCEMB, many farms in the B.C. egg industry would not be viable. If they rationalized under a competitive regime, and their numbers fell from over 200 to around 70, it would hardly be cause for an anti-combines alarm. Most economists would consider a surviving number of this magnitude to be extremely competitive.[122] Further, given that the market for many crops and products is worldwide, only a policy of foreign trade protection where the commodity is also imported could give monopoly power to domestic suppliers regardless of their size.

That farmers have accepted less than normal returns over time is a denial of their rationality and totally at variance with the evidence.[123] Creating monopolies to achieve higher returns and yet maintain larger than optimal farm populations involves slightly inconsistent policies and certainly requires more sophisticated analysis than has heretofore been given.

Of course, it could be that the general citizenry of B.C. really wants to subsidize an excess of small farmers for rural sociological/environmental purposes and can conceive no superior way to transfer supernormal incomes to those selected as worthy other than by marketing boards (and in other endeavours by crop subsidies). We are not competent to dispose of such assertions of social faith here, but we serve notice on those that advance them that we generally find their own interests rather too congruent with these policy outcomes to be fully persuasive.

Chapter IV
Policy Implications

I have never known much good done by those who affect to trade for the public good.
Smith, *Wealth of Nations*

Consumption is the sole end and purpose of all production; and the interest of the producer ought to be attended to, only so far as it may be necessary for promoting that of the consumer. The maxim is so perfectly self-evident that it would be absurd to attempt to prove it. In the mercantile system, the interest of the consumer is almost constantly sacrificed to that of the producer; and it seems to consider production and not consumption as the ultimate end and object of all industry and commerce.
Smith, *Wealth of Nations*

To expect . . . that the freedom of trade should ever be restored . . . is as absurd as to expect that an Oceana or Utopia should ever be established. . . . Not only as the prejudices of the public but what is more unconquerable, the private interests of many individuals oppose it . . . The monopoly (which many groups of producers have obtained) has so increased the number of particular tribes of them . . . that they have become formidable to the government and upon many occasions intimidate the legislation.
Smith, *Wealth of Nations*

Every monopoly which gives to a few individuals the exclusive power of carrying on certain branches of industry, is thus established in direct violation of the property of other individuals.
J.R. McCulloch, *The Principles of Political Economy*

56

Whether or not the current BCEMB/CEMA regime should be ended or continued has not been settled by our finding that significant waste is associated with it. Many public programs persist because benefits not counted by economists are overlooked (not the least of which is the election or re-election of various sponsoring legislators and parties). We hold, nonetheless, that if the ends of the program are transfers of income to "worthy" farmers, more efficient means can be employed.

A direct subsidy to egg farmers over time[124] or a lump sum, once-and-for-all payment, financed by provincial and federal taxes, makes more sense, in our opinion. Indirect payments in the form of at least an 11 cents per dozen monopoly mark-up on fresh eggs, accompanied by all the producer related inefficiencies previously mentioned, mean that every $1 of net extra income transferred by the BCEMB and CEMA to producers now costs consumers slightly over $1.25 and costs producers themselves perhaps as much as 65 cents. Furthermore, the consumers' contribution to this transfer is financed by an extraordinarily regressive "tax," since, as income increases, the number of dozens of fresh eggs consumed rises most negligibly.[125] This means that the implicit tax levied to support producers is no less regressive in practice than if a poll tax of almost $10 per family had been levied on B.C. residents, with its proceeds earmarked to existing egg producers. Surely members of a society which devotes so much political consideration to the economic defence of the poor must wonder at the inequality of such a tax, even if they do not question the distribution of its proceeds.[126]

If we are correct and the egg boards serve nothing but an inefficient redistributive role, the questions become, how much ought to be paid egg producers to give up these marketing agencies and how ought it to be financed, since inappropriate methods of compensation distribution and its financing could conceivably cause as much distortion to efficiency and create as many inequities as the current BCEMB/CEMA scheme?

First, as for means of finance, the tax that would do the least damage to wealth creation would be a poll tax; but this is, as we have just pointed out, very regressive. Much less regressive is a payment financed by the personal income tax, but neither is it without social cost. Still, it is unlikely that the social cost of securing $1 of transfers from this source would be almost 50 cents, the social cost of the current marketing board system. It is more likely to be around 15 or 25 cents.[127]

Still unsettled is how much subsidy ought to be given. If the farmers were fully reimbursed for the current value of their quota held, currently well over $1,500 a case (in 1980 dollars), they would be made better off by more than would be necessary. (Remember, this is the present value of the monopoly mark-up over all eggs sold.) If both BCEMB and CEMA were removed, competitive behaviour would ensue, producer waste decline and accrue as rent to farmers, and the assessments for administration of the boards would be avoided. Since this waste was shown to be almost half the monopoly profits, a payment of around $800 (current dollars) per case would leave producers *on average* no worse off than under the present system. We stress *on average*, since currently some small marginal firms would realize the highest decrease in unit costs under competition. Many, however, would be wiped out by the currently quota "grandfathered" farms, whose large size would have a decided advantage when competition is permitted. Perhaps a better method is to totally compensate farmers for the first 200 or 300 cases of quota per farm and thereafter at a gradually declining rate to zero dollars at 500 or 600 cases. The small firms that would undoubtedly be driven out by the ensuing competition would be no worse off, and the medium sized firms would make up in efficiency gains from economic expansion what they lost in that part of their quota value confiscated. The largest firms, already at their optimal scale, would suffer confiscation of several thousands of dollars each, but this might be ethically justified on the grounds that they realized higher than average monopoly profits under the BCEMB and CEMA. Further, some adjustment might be made depending on how recently quota was acquired. Clearly, the means of settlement is complicated, and anything short of full compensation on quota value will likely leave some firms worse off. The exact amount and method of compensation (especially its per farm limits) is a nice question of practical political economy we will leave to others to work out in detail.

Some readers who may agree that the BCEMB and CEMA ought to be eliminated will, no doubt, object to the payment of any compensation. We do not require potential victims of felonies to compensate criminals, nor are businessmen who lose wealth because of a change in technology or public tastes guaranteed relief. Why then should we compensate farmers for not using their monopoly power? In fact, some economists hold that such compensation encourages the formation of monopoly, since, once created, full compensation ensures the gains are in perpetuity. Its confiscation, therefore, has a desirable deterrent on future monopoly formation. Monopoly profits that can be truncated by political whim are much less secure, hence investment in the seeking of political support for such restrictions will be reduced.

While recognizing that compensation is a form of political tribute, we also recognize that noncompensation is a form of public confiscation. Consider that some egg farmers who recently purchased their quota earn no monopoly rents at all. Their rents were captured by the original quota owners who sold them these rights. These latter individuals currently may be enjoying the proceeds on the beach at Maui or on the golf links at Palm Springs. Of course, the real question to ask is whether the current owners who purchased quota did so with the risk of their confiscation in mind properly assessed. We know of no way to assess whether the probability distributions held by new purchasers accurately track the actual distributions of risk.[128] Undiscounted takings will appear to the recent quota purchaser as a confiscation. This has two unfortunate effects.

First, it will strengthen the notion that the public sector

is capricious in its treatment of legitimate investors. It suggests that policy is unstable. Second, and more important, it will surely be resisted. If the net loss of a unit of quota is $800 when all cost savings from a free market are concerned, quota holders can be expected to expend significant sums in order to avoid large capital losses. Purchasing quota rights may be cheaper socially and, perhaps, the only feasible way to gain the acquiescence of their owners. That the latter had the political power to gain their current advantage is an empirical fact; that this power will not be totally neutralized by the public's sudden awareness that it has been used to their disadvantage should be as apparent. Recognition of this differential power seems merely prudent to us.

Of course, various groups, the CAC, most economists, and probably the general public, will view this compensation as immoral, the recipients as largely undeserving and venal.[129] We leave the reader to decide whether selective confiscation is or is not good public policy, since we are assured that no definitive answer has yet been reached in courts, legislatures, or in scholarly musings over the subject. The question deserves more of the reader's attention than we have been able to give it here.[130]

Before we end on this ambivalent note we would like to comment briefly on one suggested alternative reform to the dismantling of the BCEMB and CEMA. The CAC stands foursquare behind the notion of marketing boards, but with the important proviso that consumers' representatives and other nonproducer representatives serve on them, perhaps in a majority status.[131] In effect, the CAC suggests we treat the production and marketing of food in Canada like a regulated public utility. This novel proposal deserves our attention, if not endorsement.

One ought to ask what forces will ensure that the general interests of consumers will be represented by the CAC or other similar public interest groups? Will the representatives be elected by consumers much as members of the current boards are elected by egg farmers? Also, how will this member (these members) know what consumer interest to serve? To assume all consumers have identical interests is clearly naïve.[132]

We do not question the good faith of the CAC or any public interest group in seeking consumer representation on regulatory commissions. The public interest, however, is very difficult to assess, while private interests are ever thrust before decision makers. General, unrepresented consumer interests—especially those of the casual product user, the poor and the less educated—are almost never given much weight, since they attract few social and political entrepreneurs. The exception is in the marketplace where these diffuse groups' dollar votes get the proportional representation and attention lost in the political arena.

Again, we do not insist that the practical difficulties and political realities in reading consumer demands by consumer advocates for various controls, price structures, grades, health standards, and the like, prove that such an alteration over the current regime is undesirable. We cannot equivocally say this. We will predict, however, that because a low cost political monitoring device is not (yet) available to the general public, the consumer advocate will overrepresent special subclasses of consumers,[133] as well as the parochial, bureaucratic interests of his or her own staff.[134]

One other proposal bears mentioning. Many writers argue that a marketing board should be permitted if it regulates supply for stabilization purposes and if a long-run competitive, cost efficient outcome is imposed. How this could be done is an interesting question, and we invite our colleagues in law, agriculture, economics, and government to work out the institutional details. We see three inherent difficulties we will share with the reader.

First of all, if a marketing board is to act as an efficient market stabilizer, it must be able to anticipate future prices more accurately than does the market. Why would a government agency have more incentive to get and disseminate this information more effectively than a market? Unless it can and will do so, there is no advantage to collectivizing the speculative functions of even imperfect futures' markets.

Second, how will the presence of monopoly be detected? If quota is given at zero price, how will supply management for stabilization be accommodated? If anyone is permitted to enter, but output quota limits are imposed on each willing producer, how are quotas to be allocated? If monopoly power is endemic to producer dominated boards, will the profits be dissipated by large numbers of excessively small firms—what economists call the open-cartel problem—since entry would continue until scale diseconomies exhaust monopoly profits?[135]

Third, how does society monitor such boards to see that they are efficient stabilizing agents that encourage efficiency in production and competitive price over the long run? Can anyone name a governmental board regulating any product operating anyplace in the world that successfully stabilizes prices and yet avoids both monopoly and production inefficiency? We are unaware of one, though we spent no little time in search.

On the whole, the record of regulation has been abysmal in promoting the welfare of consumers. As Irving Kristol recently said, no reasonable person would, in principle, be opposed to all government regulation, yet neither should all regulation be lightly assented to, given its well-known propensities toward the creation of monopoly, special interest serving, and just plain damn foolishness.[136] When regulation is of a very general sort (weights and measures, general health and safety), or when it is confined to a fairly local government level, it is not likely to become the target of special interest takeovers. When the regulation is potentially discriminatory, it will surely be exercised in a discriminatory fashion, an application of Lord Acton's well-known "theorem." There well might be a stamp affixed upon all such contemplated controls: *caveat civis*—citizen beware.

Those open minded individuals contemplating the choice between the current or amended version of the BCEMB/CEMA scheme, the multi-interest board suggested by the CAC's proposal, or a free market in eggs, should recognize that no institution will be ideal in the sense of lacking serious fault in realizing all social ends. Since all will fail in certain ways, the choice is that which is least costly in realizing all the direct and indirect gains from a product's production and distribution. We sincerely hope that the BCEMB, CEMA, and other Canadian institutions that regulate agriculture, manufacturing, services (including labour), and trade will be given greater scrutiny so that citizens and their representatives have better information on which to base their decisions on how future economic choice in these areas can be resolved.

Notes

1   In a previous draft we have been criticized by foes of marketing boards for being too conservative in our loss calculation and too feeble in our recommendations for their abolition or drastic overhaul. Friends of such agencies have accused us of unprofessional, flagrant advocacy of the free market. We hope this indicates to the general reader that we have cleaved to the centre path.

2   In 1976 there were 109, but only 88 in 1964, according to the Bank of Nova Scotia, "Marketing Boards in Canada," *Monthly Review* (January 1977). The number for 1972 was only 89, according to G.A. Hiscocks and T.A. Bennett, "Marketing Boards and Pricing in Canada," *Canadian Farm Economics* (June 1974). Campbell R. McConnell and William Henry Pope, *Economics: First Canadian Edition* (Toronto: McGraw-Hill Ryerson, 1978), claim the current number to be 130.

3   J.D. Forbes *et al., A Report on Consumer Interest in Marketing Boards*, prepared for the Canadian Consumers' Council (September 1974). *Agriculture Canada, Orientation of Canadian Agriculture: A Task Force Report* (Ottawa, 1977) claims the figure to be 60 percent for 1976. *Canada Year Book 1978-79* (Statistics Canada: Ottawa, 1979) gives the upper bound estimate.

4   V.O. Key, Jr., *Politics, Parties and Pressure Groups*, 4th ed. (New York: Thomas Y. Crowell, 1958).

5   Bank of Nova Scotia, "Marketing Boards in Canada."

6   As legal scholars well know, the impact of this movement on American legal thinking has been dramatic. In the five *Granger cases* decided by the U.S. Supreme Court in 1877, particularly *Munn* v. *Illinois* (94 U.S. 113), the Court turned about in its view of

the limits of state intervention. Despite the then orthodox interpretation of the restriction on the individual states' use of their regulatory authority by the Constitution's interstate commerce provision, the Court ruled that the laws of certain Midwestern states setting transport and storage tariff schedules (or charge maximums) were within the ambit of the police powers of the individual states. The Court stated that private property which has putative economic spillover on the rest of the community was "affected with a public interest," and "must submit to be controlled by the public for the common good." One hundred years later the limits on the "public interest" are still debated. On this see Bernard Schwartz, *Law in America* (New York: American Heritage Society, 1974) or Clair Wilcox and William G. Shepherd, *Public Policies toward Business*, 5th ed. (Homewood, Illinois: Richard C. Irwin, 1975). Interestingly enough, the reasoning behind the *Granger cases* control Canadian jurisprudential discussions of regulation, too, according to regulatory scholar Professor Hudson Janisch of the University of Toronto's Faculty of Law.

7   J.A.E. Morley, "Marketing Boards," in T.K. Warley (ed.), *Agricultural Producers and Their Markets* (New York: Augustus Kelley, 1967). Margaret Digby and R.H. Gretton, *Co-operative Marketing for Agricultural Producers* (Rome: U.N. Food and Agricultural Organization, 1977) also confirm that marketing boards were born in Queensland, Australia, but fail to say in what activity supply was restricted. Richard Albion informed us that this first board was formed to regulate the supply of wheat.

8   W.M. Drummond, W.J. Anderson, and T.C. Kerr, *A Review of Agricultural Policy in Canada* (Ottawa: Agricultural Research Council of Canada, 1966).

There is a wide and hoary literature on co-ops and their notorious instability. It appears their high mortality rate is based on two facts: first, the market for inputs they compete with is more competitive than is generally realized by the hopeful founders of co-ops; second, middlemen-type functions are costly to carry out, and much skill is required to effect an efficient coordination. The incentives for nonprofit co-op managers and individual members to bear risk and invest in information with uncertain payoffs is considerably less than it is in the profit-oriented firms that co-ops hope to supplant. Even with significant tax advantages, the co-op movement exhibits far from an unbroken record of successes.

9   Drummond, *A Review of Agricultural Policy in Canada*.

10 Drummond, *A Review of Agricultural Policy in Canada*. Drummond claims that Section 121 of the *B.N.A. Act* prohibits restrictions on interprovincial trade, and Section 91 gives control of commerce to the federal government. Things become complicated, however, since primary responsibility in agricultural policy and civil rights, Sections 95 and 93 respectively, is shared by both levels of government.

11 Bank of Nova Scotia, "Marketing Boards in Canada."

12 An outstanding discussion of the U.S. experience is to be found in Ellis W. Hawley, *The New Deal and the Problem of Monopoly* (Princeton, New Jersey: Princeton University Press, 1966).

13 A.W. Wood *et al.*, *Market Regulation in Canadian Agriculture* (Department of Agricultural Economics and Farm Manager, University of Manitoba, May 1972).

14 McConnell and Pope, *Economics*. They claim that Quebec had no agricultural boards until 1958. Newfoundland, which did not join the Confederation until 1949, had no boards until CEMA was created in 1972. Also see Wood, *Market Regulation in Canadian Agriculture*.

15 Hawley, *The New Deal and the Problem of Monopoly*.

16 Wood, *Market Regulation in Canadian Agriculture*. For a short discussion of the constitutional problems involved in marketing boards see A.E. Safarian, *Canadian Federalism and Economic Integration* (Ottawa: Queen's Printer, 1974).

17 Bank of Nova Scotia, "Marketing Boards in Canada." It should be clear without resort to formal proof that a provincial marketing board's inability to prohibit imports severely restricts its ability to raise prices above the competitive level. As the noted specialists in the area, P.T. Bauer and B.S. Yamey, have pointed out in "The Economics of Marketing Reform," *Journal of Political Economy* (June 1954), in many cases the function of marketing boards is limited to acting as state "marketing agent" which levies a disguised tax. In other cases it involves only the regulation of terms of sale, place of sale, and product quality, or it provides information and technical advice. Political lobbying for subsidies from the government, and advertising and other promotional activity are yet other non-cartel purposes of marketing boards. Thus, the Canadian Wheat Board plays this role of agent to market Canadian wheat and other grains, but given world supply conditions, it clearly has no ability to affect world prices. Its function is purely as middleman and speculator, although it represents Prairie farmers' interests in one way or another when it sets the domestic prices it pays under the Grain Stabilization Act.

18 The "war" erupted in 1970 when Manitoba and Ontario began shipping "surplus" eggs into Quebec with predictable results to prices and egg farm incomes within that province. The latter retaliated by "dumping" surplus broiler chickens in Ontario. Quebec also set up a marketing board for distribution of all eggs in its own province which discriminated against "foreign" eggs. Ontario retorted via an attempt to block sales of Quebec broilers by Ontario retailers. The Manitoba and the federal supreme courts found the provinces lacked power to unilaterally restrict interprovincial importations, and so Parliament, facing a very difficult interprovincial and constitutional squabble, settled for Bill C-176.

19 It should be noted, however, that while Canada was strengthening its marketing boards, Britain, because of severe political pressures upon the Consumers' Committee and the Committee of Investigation of Parliament, began to rethink her position. In the Agriculture Act of 1970 the British Egg Marketing Board was dissolved [G.R. Allen, *Agricultural Marketing Policies* (Oxford: Blackwell, 1958)]. It ought also to be pointed out that the British Egg Marketing Board operated in a quite different way from CEMA and the BCEMB. The British system involved per-dozen subsidies and few supply or entry restrictions. On this we have been enlightened by A.G.A. Fisher, "A Study in Agricultural Marketing: A Different View of Orderly Marketing" (paper presented at Poultry Industry Conference, Eastbourne, U.K., October 1967).

20 The objectives of the federal agencies (only CEMA initially) created to coordinate provincial boards were, according to the 1972 law's preamble, "to promote a strong, efficient and competitive producing and marketing industry for the regulated product or products . . . and to have due regard to the interests of the producers and consumers of the regulated product or products."

21 Theoretically, the NFPMC has enormous powers over the national boards. For one, they can reject a national board's decision. Currently, they have placed "sunset" rules on the latter's pronouncements. Thus, all current CEMA rulings must be reviewed and put in place again in a specified time period or they lose their legal force. Much of my information on NFPMC comes from conversation with John Berry of the [Canadian] Anti-Inflation Board and from reading James Forbes' works. Particularly useful is Forbes, "Insuring Public Accountability and Consumer Interest in Regulatory Agencies in the Food Industry," Working Paper No. 399, Faculty of Commerce and Business Administration, University of British Columbia, July 1976.

22 Separate legislation prior to Bill C-176 had already created as Crown corporations the Canadian Dairy Commission (1966) and Canadian Wheat Board (1935). They both differ from those permitted under Bill C-176 in that their directors are all government appointed, not producer elected (Bank of Nova Scotia, "Marketing Boards in Canada").

23 Two typical examples of this thinking are the pronouncements of CEMA in its *Newsletter* (November 1973) and the statement of the then and now federal Minister of Agriculture, Eugene Whelan, in the Report of the Special Committee on Egg Marketing, Issue No. 2, *Egg Marketing* (Ottawa: Queen's Printer, 1972). They are also discussed by Geoffrey Hiscocks, "Theory and Evolution of Agricultural Market Regulations in Canada," in *Market Regulations in Canadian Agriculture* (Winnipeg: Department of Agricultural Economics, University of Manitoba, May 1972) and in F.W. Beeson (ed.), *Canadian Poultryman* (New Westminster, B.C.: Farm Papers, April 1973). They are discussed at length and in some detail in a

worldwide context by Bauer and Yamey, "The Economics of Marketing Reform."

24 From the *Farm Products Marketing Act* of 1972, Canadian Egg Marketing Agency Proclamation, *The Canadian Gazette, Part II, Statutory Instruments,* Vol. 107 (Ottawa: Queen's Printer, 1973). The provincial boards have never seen fit to appoint nonproducers, nor has Cabinet reached outside the industry for CEMA representatives.

25 In terms of the entire Canadian market, B.C. gets approximately 12 percent of the nation's total domestic supply. A trivial amount equal to less than 1 percent of the latter is imported from abroad. CEMA does not directly control these imports, but since 1974 these foreign eggs are "coordinated" into the domestic market through import quotas issued by the Department of Industry, Trade and Commerce.

26 Conversations with James Forbes confirm this, but it is clear that given the small tariff on breakers coming into Canada—currently only 15 cents per pound in powdered form—and the fact that Canada is probably a net exporter of processed eggs (to be discussed in Chapter III), CEMA's pricing power is considerably less in its dealings in this area, as opposed to the fresh market, although CEMA organizes all domestic contracts in the former. Thus, as a first approximation we will assume the Canadian breaker market is "workably competitive," though the junior researcher in this project and John Berry are not quite as sanguine, given government domestic interventions. They both agree, however, that such interventions are severely curtailed, given the high elasticities for this market, both worldwide and domestic.

27 Currently (1978) the CEMA levy is 4½ cents and the BCEMB another 1½ cents per dozen. The latter is for administration, while the former covers "surplus removals," and CEMA's administration, including advertising and what are referred to as "legitimate lobbying activities."

28 B.C. actually served notice to drop out of CEMA in 1973, and in 1974 the BCEMB again threatened to leave. At both times Manitoba, Quebec, and Ontario were running large surpluses, and tales of over 25 million rotting eggs in 1974—probably no great exaggeration—filled Canadian newspapers. B.C. egg farmers believed, and quite correctly so, that their contributions toward the CEMA equalization funds were subsidizing their eastern counterparts, since B.C. was running no surplus. CEMA, faced with claims that exceeded its resources, adjusted its payments downward. It paid only 85 percent of the wholesale price for surplus eggs and raised its levies from the original level of 1 cent per dozen. It appears that since 1974 the national board levies have covered outlays.

29 One representative must come from each of Vancouver Island and

the B.C. Interior Region, respectively, while the remaining two must be chosen from farmers in the Lower Mainland region. Other provincial boards are chosen on roughly the same principles to ensure that the area with the greatest number of members does not dominate all positions. Actually, in August of 1976 the B.C. Minister of Agriculture dissolved the board, which then consisted of five producers, and appointed members by Cabinet Order. This position was reversed in March of 1977. There was much contention over this move, since consumer advocates wished nonproducer interests to be represented.

30   Discussions with BCEMB officials.

31   Sixty-nine birds over 24 months of age per annual weekly case was the initial ruling. This has since changed to 71 birds over 20 months of age per annual weekly case.

32   This is discussed in the *Canadian Consumer* (August 1977). This magazine is the bi-monthly publication of the Consumers' Association of Canada (hereafter the CAC).

33   By relative price is meant the *real* not the nominal price. The real price of a commodity is its cost at the margin to the consumer, measured in terms of other commodities foregone. As a practical matter, the real price of a commodity is its nominal price divided by the nominal price of "all other goods." The Consumer Price Index, or CPI, is one convenient approximation for the latter composite price. Thus, if the nominal price of a commodity rose, but by less than the CPI, we would say that this good or service had become less expensive in real terms, whereas we would say that real price had risen if it were the other way around.

34   Food Prices Review Board, *Report on Egg Prices* (Ottawa: 1975).

35   "An Examination of Egg Production Costs in Canada: A Report to the Canadian Egg Marketing Agency" (January 1975) and "Provincial Models of the Farm-Gate Cost of Egg Production for Medium Size Producers: A Report to the Canadian Egg Marketing Agency" (July 1975).

36   "An Examination of Egg Production Costs in Canada."

37   That the costs per dozen are based on the assumption of fixed coefficients should not of itself be taken as a serious indictment of its method. As long as the relative price input prices do not change too radically over the life of the formula—three years said CEMA in its brief answer to Forbes *et al.* in Ottawa on 25 February 1976—the upward bias of the inaccuracy is small. The discussion of change in input prices and resulting change in unit cost is slightly technical, but for small changes it can be approximated by the ratio $\frac{I}{Q}\Delta P_I$

where I is the level of the input used per unit of output, Q, at that input's price, P_I (other output prices held constant), and ΔP_I is the change in the input's cost. This intelligent man-on-the-street's approximation is exactly what P.S. Ross offered CEMA. The theoretical bases of this approximation are discussed in Paul A. Samuelson, *Foundations of Economic Analysis* (Cambridge, Mass.: Harvard University Press, 1947). Vernon W. Yorganson, "But Who Reviews the Reviewers? The Case of Eggs," *Canadian Public Policy* (Summer 1976), shows statistically (for Ontario) that this formula has been employed rather strictly. He does not establish, however, that the absolute price set by CEMA is competitive, only that the formula is more than cosmetic. Yorganson shows, interestingly enough, that product pricing in the 1969-72, pre-CEMA, post-marketing board period, closely tracked the cost formula currently used by CEMA. This would suggest that CEMA merely took over and coordinated the existing provincial boards' policies. That such carry-over did not lead to a price hike in Ontario would appear inconsistent with B.C.'s experience. Yorganson's regression equation, however, is in nominal terms, with input prices and the price level as additive independent variables. That the coefficient of the last has a positive (though statistically insignificant) coefficient means relative product price was, in fact, increasing at a higher rate than input prices in this period, since both input and wholesale product prices were generally rising.

38   Since the price of breakers is set in international markets, it is unlikely that even large numbers of eggs diverted to it can lower price there very much, except in the very short run. Forbes *et al.* cannot be correct.

39   In the U.S., in certain regions, egg producers voluntarily contribute 5 cents per case of eggs or roughly three- to four-tenths of 1 percent of the wholesale receipts to institutional advertising and promotion, largely determined by their organizations, the United Egg Producers and the American Egg Board. The levy program arranged through the U.S. Department of Agriculture applies to all operations exceeding 3,000 hens, i.e., 45 cases per week. Only 2 percent of the 10,000 producers affected by the checkoff asked to have their shares of advertising refunded [*Wall Street Journal* (29 December 1976)]. Forbes' "ideal" levy would exceed this by more than a factor of 10.

40   Letter to the CAC's counsel, Mr. T.G. Kane, from CEMA, dated 18 February 1976. Made available by James Forbes.

41   *The Vancouver Sun* (26 February 1976).

42   Also see James Forbes/CAC, "Brief to [B.C.] Select Standing Committee on Agriculture," 21 September 1977. Of course, Manitoba eggs could command only 3 percent of the B.C. market and still have 10 cents per dozen lower unit costs, but it would say something unlikely about the relative inelasticity of Manitoba egg supply as compared to B.C. Forbes is probably right when he goes on and questions how free egg movements are between provinces. Of course, this was originally recognized in Bill C-176, which was

deliberately drafted to get around provincial restrictions on imports of sister provinces' product.

43   Reported *Vancouver Sun* (26 February 1976).

44   It appears according to Forbes that the NFPMC has pursued its own study in 1977 but has not released it to the public. In Forbes/ CAC, "Briefing Notes for Meeting with the National Farm Products Marketing Council," 13 October 1977, Forbes claims that he had "been *denied* the Council's [NFPMC's] own study of egg production costs— . . . despite the facts that: (1) in its reports on the hearings, Council promised to undertake studies on fully six items in the cost of production formula . . . (2) we are aware of differences in the methods used and some of the conclusions reached in the P.S. Ross and Council studies respectively; it is not unreasonable to suspect that a study commissioned by CEMA (i.e., the P.S. Ross study) might be less objective than a public interest regulatory body. (That this is not an overly suspicious attitude for us to adopt was suggested by Paul Bakey, Chairman of the Council [NFPMC], who, in an October 7 telephone conversation said 'Council undertook its own study because it felt it would be unwise to rely totally on a producer study for a change in the formula'.)"

45   Forbes and Kerton are both marketing specialists. Forbes came to the academy with considerable business experience in the U.S. feed grain market. Kraft is an agriculture specialist.

46   Reported by Nicole Strickland in "Consumer's Corner" in *The Vancouver Province* (27 August 1976). We also obtained a copy through The Fraser Institute's good offices.

47   No one in Agriculture Canada or Cabinet has disputed the authenticity of this document.

48   The transportation and tariff figures are also based upon the James D. Forbes *et al.* testimony before the NFPMC in Ottawa on 26 February 1976 on behalf of the CAC. These are also confirmed in the DM-10 document.

49   P.S. Ross & Partners, "Provincial Models of the Farm-Gate Cost of Egg Production for Medium Size Producers: A Report to the Canadian Egg Marketing Agency."

50   It is true that 1972 presents difficulties in explanation. We have not, unfortunately, solved this puzzle. The reader may also have noticed that in 1973 the price differential fell dramatically over 1972. This is more easily explained. B.C. egg farmers, anticipating that CEMA would issue new quota prorated on flock size, dramatically increased the size of their flocks. Consequent supply enforcement problems developed in 1973. We are indebted to Forbes for this insight.

51   1975 prices are used through this section to aid in comparison with the Forbes/CAC study and government report DM-10. This is carried over into Chapter III of the study where the social costs of

the BCEMB and CEMA are estimated in 1975 dollars.

52 The difference is statistically significant well beyond the 95 percent level of confidence. There is no difference, however, in the means of relative price indices between 1968-1972—the pre-CEMA, but post-BCEMB period—and 1973-1978—the post-CEMA period. Of course, the 1972 price outlier explains this.

53 Richard Shaffner, "Canada's Import Quotas: A Case of Domestic Goals vs. International Relations," *Backgrounder No. 2* (Canadian-American Committee: Montreal and Washington, D.C., September 1975), points out that the Minister of Agriculture, Eugene Whelan, was the authority who announced the import limitation quota, although as a foreign trade measure it would have had to be administered by the Department of Industry, Trade and Commerce. Shaffner claims that although *de jure* CEMA does not control these quotas, *de facto* they receive the necessary "support" to do so indirectly. We cannot corroborate this speculation.

54 In 1968 the ratio of actual to allowable quota was 85.9 percent, this rose to 91.5 percent in 1971, but had fallen back to 85.5 percent in 1975 [1968-1973 B.C. Egg Marketing Board, *Summary of the Special Audit of Egg Production Quotas*; 1974 and 1975, Minutes of the Annual Meeting of B.C. Egg Producers (17 April 1975 and 17 March 1976)].

55 As mentioned earlier, the transfer market for quota was severely restricted in B.C. until recently. Before 1976 a new producer could enter only by buying out an existing producer's farm. The quota was attached to the farm. Also, no producer whose quota before 1968 was less than 200 cases could exceed that figure, and those who were "grandfathered" with a larger number of rights were prohibited from expansion. This limit is now 280 cases or about 20,000 birds.

56 Of course, π could move all around over time because of market instabilities. This seems highly unlikely, since the annual demand and supply conditions in eggs—though not the seasonal shifts—are thought to be very stable. Also, income elasticity of demand is probably not significantly above zero. See note 125.

57 This is an implicit price, since quota was attached to the full farm operation, land improvements and all, before 1976 [estimated by R.M.A. Loyns with A.J.W. Pursaga, *Poultry Marketing Boards and the Canadian Consumer*, Review of the Consumer Interest in the Market Regulation of Canadian Agriculture (March 1974)]. This quota value also emerged in a series of B.C. government hearings (the Garrish Report), *Report of the Independent Egg Marketing Survey* (September 1972). We have converted to 1975 prices this and all subsequent quota values unless otherwise stated.

58 Asking price listed in the B.C. Egg Marketing Board, *News Bulletin* (13 August 1976).

59 Sale price determined from reports in *The Vancouver Sun* (23 and 25

May 1977). In the 25 May report it was stated that Mr. Arnold Link, a disgruntled Prince George poultryman, sold his 200 case quota and 6,000 birds for $150,000. He had previously given away thousands of birds, the first report said, each worth $1.25. Thus, the value of the 200 cases of quota was $142,500, making quota value around $712 per case. Reduction by $12 is arbitrary, but is based on the fact that interior producers do not supply all of their market, because imports are shipped in from the Lower Mainland. Accordingly, there probably is a locational cost advantage to the Interior at present. The over-$1,000 figure is quite accurate and reflects the actual market transfer prices in late 1977, based on discussions with B.C. bankers who finance loans on quota and treat them as they would other farm related capital. Forbes' "Brief to the [B.C.] Select Standing Committee on Agriculture" cites $1,425 (1977 dollars) as quota value for mid-1977. This works out to $1,225 in 1975 dollars. We have been told by John McManus that quota in Ontario and Quebec were at least $750 in 1975 and 1976; they would be no lower in B.C., according to all of Forbes' studies, since he asserts that the level of protection offered farmers is greater in B.C.

60 Phone conversation and reported in *The Vancouver Sun* (17 November 1979).

61 A regression was first run using the actual minimum estimated quota values in 1975 dollar figures ($350, $550, and $750) as dependent variable and dates 1972, 1976, and 1977 as the respective independent variables. If the figures had been $500, $700, and $1,200, more likely numbers, the interpolated figure for 1975 would have risen from $550 to $800. Thus $675 is the average of both the low and probable 1975 estimates. Obviously, our figures have no statistical significance, but are used for purposes of interpolation. A simple average would have yielded the same figure.

62 Proposed Bill C-42 (first reading 16 March 1977) was displaced by Bill C-13 (18 November 1977). Section 4.5 in the latter, after much lobbying effort by farm organizations and provincial marketing boards, totally exempted marketing boards from the amended anti-combines proposal. See W.T. Stanbury, "Competition Policy: The Retreat Begins," *Canadian Consumer* (February 1978). Farm groups, however, are frightened by the prospect that consumer scrutiny of their actions will remove their monopoly privileges. (Stanbury states that 40 of the 147 presentations on hearings for Bill C-42 were from farm groups and provincial marketing boards, while consumer groups supplied only 3 submissions.) A casual look at the shrinking size of the Canadian farm population over time (from over one-third at the turn of the century to about one-twentieth today) suggests that agriculture's political power may at some point vanish. That this is happening in the U.S., where controls (usually different from Canada's) are gradually being dismantled, is clear. See the essays of American agriculturalists D. Gale Johnson *et al.*, *Food and Agricultural Policy* (Washington, D.C.: American Enterprise Institute for Public Policy Research, 1977).

63 The reader will recall that the market for eggs has two segments, fresh and breaker (or processed). This complication causes no problem, however, in the estimation of π, for the following reasons: the total monopoly profit for the marginal firm permitted to belong to the cartel is the sum of receipts from breaker and fresh markets less the aggregate of production costs to effect these sales. It follows, therefore, that at the margins of decisions, $\pi = \theta P_f + (1-\theta)P_b - S_m$, where θ is the share of fresh to total egg production and the subscripts refer to the fresh and breaker submarkets. Since the farm gate price, P, is a "blend" equal to $\theta P_f + (1-\theta)P_b$, it necessarily follows that π is $P - S_m$. Compositing eggs of both submarkets and calling them Q, therefore, causes no great difficulty, though it is necessary to consider θ as a technical given, which it is not. Allowing θ to vary in our analysis for Chapter III would, however, add a level of complication outweighed by returns. We have, in fact, done this, and the social cost differences that emerge are of a trivial magnitude.

64 No doubt there will be those who will view the monopoly rights as permanent, but they will hardly dominate the margins of purchase. Actually, each producer, extant and potential, will have a probability distribution of "durability" in mind. It seems as likely, though we cannot prove it, that the marginal purchaser thinks the monopoly has a 2 year future life span as a 20 year duration. At discount rates from 8 to 12 percent this means that π ranges from 5.6 to 30.5 cents, if such a distribution includes no other possibilities. This range gives an average of 18 cents for the difference between price and unit cost. Thus the 11 cent estimate is hardly excessive on this score.

65 Forbes/CAC testimony, 26 February 1976. It should as well be noted that the Agricultural Economics Research Council of Canada's study "The Cost of Canada's Egg System" (January 1979) gives B.C. quota rental price in the range 13 to 19 cents (in 1975 dollars) for the year 1978.

66 Forbes/CAC presentation 26 February 1976, and Forbes *et al., A Report on Consumer Interest in Marketing Boards* (Ottawa: Consumer Research Council Report No. 1, September 1974). All columnists in Canada seem to do so as well. We might have argued that this suggests the high social returns to inviting journalists back to university (at public expense!) in the name of "economic literacy," but this might be interpreted as both arrogant and self-serving.

67 Between 1968 and 1975, when outright sales of quota were prohibited, the number of producers somehow managed to halve while output declined only slightly, less than 5 percent. Clearly merger was permitted, though not unlimited, allowing the integration of land, plant, and operation. Yoram Barzel and Christopher Hall, *The Oil Import Quota* (Stanford, California: The Hoover Institution of War, Revolution and Peace, 1976), show this is a device used in the U.S. import oil market to reduce cost and raise profit in the face of restriction of outright quota sales.

68 If the monopolist was originally in equilibrium, the additional cost of a unit of output equals the additional revenue. After the cost increase, however, this former would exceed the latter. Assuming that incremental costs increase with output, but marginal revenue is negatively related, it follows that anything which causes the cost of production to rise at the margins will cause output to be reduced. As was earlier discussed, restriction on quota transferal raises cost to the group as a whole. Since this raises marginal cost as well, one would predict that output would decline as a result. In Figure 1 restrictions on transferability of quota cause the group supply function, S, to rise. If Q_m, the chosen output, was, previous to the prohibition, the group's preferred output, the cost increase would lead to a smaller output. No doubt, mark-up theories of pricing, which appeal to the man on the street, underlie the CAC's position. Mark-up theories, however, beg the question of what determines the mark-up factor. Price differentials are market determined, not determining.

69 In Chapter II, we discussed how monopoly profits get capitalized into present or asset values. This means that some current owners paid past owners the value of the monopoly profits for the foreseeable future. Thus, many current owners earn only a normal return. It is just as if the current users rented the monopoly rights from the previous owners.

70 Readers acquainted with the works of James Buchanan, Gordon Tullock, John Rawls, and Robert Nozick will be familiar with this "expected valuation" method of comparing situations where gains and losses do not move in the same direction for all individuals. Instead of specific allocative states being compared, the payoffs for streams of action under alternative rules are considered. A rule of law permitting monopoly in this world is found undesirable, since its expected value to the representative citizen is less than one of not allowing or at least discouraging such behaviour. A nice summary of this "contractarian" approach to cost/benefit welfare analysis is found in Charles K. Rowley and Alan T. Peacock, *Welfare Economics: A Liberal Restatement* (London: Martin Robinson, 1975).

71 Of course, such goals or ends are not the only things politicians consider, but they clearly are concerned about them in an indirect way. They individually strive to represent particular interests, but realize through their mutual interaction with agents of other groups that compromise is required. Such compromises take on the character of exchanges which *crudely* approximate an attempt to maximize community wealth with due allowance for the imperfections attendant to this process. Unfortunately, key groups often find themselves unrepresented in this "logrolling" process. On this see James M. Buchanan and Gordon Tullock, *The Calculus of Consent: Logical Foundations of Constitutional Democracy* (Ann Arbor: University of Michigan Press, 1962).

72 For instance, Ronald J. Wonnacott and Paul Wonnacott, *Free Trade between the United States and Canada* (Cambridge, Mass.: Harvard University Press, 1967), claim that the tariff reduced Canadians' income in aggregate by 10 percent, and, in *Looking Outward* (Ottawa: Information Canada, 1975), the Economic Council of Canada admitted it to be at least 5 percent. Richard A. Posner, "The Social Costs of Monopolies and Regulation," *Journal of Political Economy* (August 1975), argues that monopoly may cost the American economy as much as 2 or 3 percent of real incomes. Brookings Institution Senior Fellow, Edward F. Denison, in "Effects of Selected Changes in the Institutional and Human Environment upon Output per Unit of Input," U.S. Department of Commerce, *Survey of Current Business* (January 1978), estimates that environmental health and safety regulations decrease the current U.S. income by almost 1.5 percent and reduce the rate of growth by almost one-half a percentage point. (Had such factors as lower growth been operative since the turn of the century in the U.S. or Canada, real incomes today would have been approximately one-quarter to one-third lower than they actually are.) Murray L. Weidenbaum and Robert DeFina, *The Cost of Federal Regulation of Economic Activity* (Washington, D.C.: American Enterprise Institute for Public Policy Research, May 1968), estimate that the U.S. federal safety, environmental, energy, and "industry specific" regulations absorb 4 percent of GNP. Neither Denison nor Weidenbaum and DeFina measure even crudely what fraction of this is economic "waste," but it is probably a nonnegligible percentage. A nice summary is found by Weidenbaum in "Estimating Regulatory Costs," *Regulation* (May/June 1978). Richard Zerbe and Nichole Urban, "Toward a Public Interest Theory of Regulation," *Research in Law and Economics* (forthcoming 1981) indicate that about half of social regulation is wasteful. Putting all of these together, it would not be outrageous to say that tariffs, monopoly restraints, and uneconomic regulation waste 10 percent of Canadian GNP. In current terms (1980 incomes and prices) this amounts to some $3,000 per family, a significant loss to say the very least.

73 The senior author is fond of rigorously demonstrating in his classes the theorem that the economic gains to monopoly producers are less than the losses to consumers. He then asks whether the monopoly concessions in public buildings in the U.S. and Canada which are given to blind and maimed veterans of past wars to sell magazines, soft drinks, candy, cigarettes, and such, ought to be turned over to competitive suppliers and the disabled veterans pensioned off or set to making brooms or even begging. Clearly, external benefits of a program to individual citizens other than consumers of the monopolized service might militate against this solution. Put another way, all income transfers schemes have misallocative consequences, and these are best thought of as the various costs of doing the public's business.

74 We are assuming now that the prices of the factors used by the industry reflect more or less accurately their social values elsewhere. Presence of pollution, for instance, in producing the good would probably violate this assumption, since the firms are "purchasing," at zero cost to themselves, part of the environment and degrading it. Since the marginal value to consumers of a clean environment is hardly zero, such an "uncompensated taking," to use the legal term, would mean that the market supply price of the good understates its social cost. We do not consider this to be a problem for eggs. Of course, if monopoly were important in other industries from which factors also used to produce eggs are purchased, the factors could be priced too low, reflecting not their worth in other uses but what the monopolized industries have to pay. In such a case, the supply curve would again understate the social costs of expansion. For eggs, the possibilities of factors being priced too low seem somewhat remote. Almost 80 percent of private costs are in grain and capital expenses, both of which are set in competitive international markets. Labour, the most suspect price, is only 5 percent of costs. We doubt the price of laying hens, another important and internationally traded input, is distorted much either. Land rents are made too low because of other agriculture monopoly distortions and restrictions on residential developments; but since land is such a minor factor of production in eggs, this distortion is of small consequence, too. In short, we assert with some confidence that the costs borne by egg producers reflect more or less the social costs of their output. On the question of distortions elsewhere mitigating or enlarging the welfare losses due to a particular set of impediments in the market in question, see the section on welfare measurements in Arnold C. Harberger's collection, *Taxation and Welfare* (Boston: Little, Brown and Company, 1974).

75 Consumers incompetent to monitor the quantity or quality of a commodity would seriously compromise this assumption. For eggs, however, it seems safe to say that, given the aid of grading standards, the consumer can shop for them unaided by either the state or even the CAC. Put bluntly, if they cannot competently purchase eggs, can they be expected to choose their elected representatives with any care?

76 Again, consumer price-taking is assumed. That is, each consumer believes his own behaviour has no measurable effect on the price charged; hence, the perceived marginal acquisition cost is the market price.

77 When price falls from β to P_c, more of the commodity will be purchased because consumers substitute for the commodity with the lower price. The same effect occurs because the consumer is also wealthier; as the price falls, measured real income increases by the amount $(- \Delta P \cdot Q_c)$, which means that the consumption value placed on the output is also affected by this income effect. If the latter were to be removed, consumers would be poorer, hence they

would not buy Q_c, but somewhat less. Thus, saying they would pay area $OQ_cB\beta$ for Q_c rather than do without it is an overstatement, since $OQ_cB\beta$ is predicted partially at least on the higher real income from the price fall from β to P_c. In eggs this overstatement is virtually zero, since the effect of price change on real income is trivially small for the changes that we will consider. More importantly, empirical evidence indicates that a person's consumption is fairly invariant to changes in income. On this, see note 123. Thus, we can confidently neglect this income effect, and demand curve βD can safely be used as a measure of consumer welfare in dollar terms.

78   Arnold C. Harberger's classic work, "Monopoly and Resource Allocation," *American Economic Review* (May 1954), was the first and perhaps the most famous study to measure the aggregate cost of monopoly in terms of triangle measures. Harberger came up with the totally trivial loss figure of one-tenth of 1 percent of GNP for the U.S. Recently, that figure has been raised to one-half of 1 percent by Dean A. Worcester, "New Estimates of the Welfare Loss to Monopoly, United States: 1956-1969," *Southern Economic Journal* (October 1973). It should be clear that this part of monopoly, the distortion caused by producing too little of one thing and too much of another, is not particularly damaging.

79   Price elasticity is equal to $\dfrac{\Delta Q}{Q} \div \dfrac{\Delta P}{P}$, where Δ means "change in." In words, this is the percentage change in quantity divided by the percentage change in price. The area of the triangle ABD is half the product of its base times its height or $\frac{1}{2}\pi\Delta Q$, where ΔQ refers to the change in Q, $Q_c - Q_m$ and equals $(\dfrac{\Delta P}{P} \cdot Q_m \cdot \eta)$, where ΔP is the fall in price from P_m to P_c. Now if $\Delta P'$ is the rise in supply cost from P'_m to P_c as output expands, ΔQ, it should be obvious that $\pi = \Delta P' - \Delta P$. Therefore,

$$\Delta P = (\frac{\Delta P}{\Delta P' - \Delta P}) \cdot \pi.$$

By multiplying the numerator and denominator of $(\dfrac{\Delta P}{\Delta P' - \Delta P})$ by $(\dfrac{Q_m}{P_m \Delta Q})$, we obtain

$$\Delta P = \frac{1/\eta}{\left(\dfrac{P_m}{P'_m}\right)\dfrac{1}{\sigma} - \dfrac{1}{\eta}} = (\frac{\sigma'}{\sigma' - \eta}) \cdot \pi$$

where $\sigma' = (\dfrac{P_m}{P'_m})\sigma$. The elasticities hold only at the point Q_m, so W_T is very accurate only when ΔQ is small. To become more accurate, we would have to use actual specifications of the demand and supply functions and integrate them over the range Q_m to Q_c. Alternatively, we could convert the formulation of W_T into arc-elasticity terms. The former requires the use of functions of dubious econometric accuracy. The latter involves laborious algebraic calculations requiring solving a quadratic equation for ΔP and inserting one of its roots into a messy form for ΔQ. The increase in accuracy is small and, given the estimation range of η and σ, seems to us an uneconomic presentation. The reader should also note that our formulation is relatively standard—for all the above reasons—and was originally suggested by T. Dudley Wallace, "Measures of Social Cost of Agricultural Programs," *American Journal of Agricultural Economics* (May 1962). Another apparent alternative, however, involves the conversion of elasticity estimates and knowledge of P_m, P'_m, and Q_m into linear demand supply approximation $P_d = a + bQ$ and $P_s = c + dQ$, where P_c and P_s are the respective demand and supply prices for a given Q. As can easily be demonstrated,

$$a = P_m \left(1 + \frac{1}{\eta}\right), \quad b = \frac{P_m}{\eta Q_m}, \quad c = P'_m \left(1 + \frac{1}{\sigma}\right) \text{ and } d = \frac{P'_m}{\sigma Q_m}.$$

This method is employed by A.C. Beck, "The Social Cost of Production Control in the Australian Egg Industry," *Review of Marketing and Agricultural Economics* (December 1974) and by Herbert G. Grubel and Richard W. Schwindt, *The Real Cost of the B.C. Milk Board: A Case Study in Canadian Agricultural Policy* (Vancouver, B.C.: The Fraser Institute, 1977). The reader should note that this technique is not conceptually different from ours and yields about the same results.

80 William G. Tamek and Kenneth Robinson, *Agricultural Product Prices* (Ithaca, New York: Cornell University Press, 1972), note the long-run demand elasticities are often twice or three times their short-run level. They suggest $\eta = -0.6$. Linda Whetstone's "A Free Market for Eggs," in *Essays in the Theory of Pricing* (London: Institute of Economic Affairs, 1967) survey for Britain and Europe found η between -0.25 and -0.50. R.M.A. Loyns and W.F. Lu, "Characteristics of Demand for Eggs in Canada: An Analysis of Cross-Section and Time Series Data" (Department of Agriculture, University of Manitoba, September 1972), estimate η at -1.0, but Z. Hassan and S.R. Johnson, "The Demand for Major Foods in Canada," *Canadian Farm Economics* (April 1977), find $\eta = -0.12$. Beck, "The Social Cost of Production Control," reports a range of -0.23 to -0.32 for Australia. D.S. Sidhu, *Demand and Supply of Eggs: An Econometric Analysis* (New Delhi: S. Chand and Company, 1974), exhaustively surveys U.S. and U.K. studies and offers η's of between -0.24 and -1.5.

81 R.M.A. Loyns and W.F. Lu, "Characteristics of Demand for Eggs in Canada." Other studies cannot be used, since characteristics of the production functions differ markedly in B.C. from those in U.S. and other markets, with the exception, no doubt, of the U.S. Pacific Northwest. Agricultural economists point out that one pitfall in estimating σ is concentrating on existing farm units, as is typical in cross-section data, instead of on output behaviour allowing for entry

and exit. Also for the long run, input prices change sufficiently, as does technology, so insensitivity of output product to price changes may involve serious specification problems. Common sense clearly indicates σ exceeds $+1.0$. We owe this discussion to the vigorous arguments of Donald F. Gordon and John Berry, who hold the ordinary measures for σ to be seriously biased on the low side.

82 For 1975 Statistics Canada found 2.5 million persons living in B.C. with 3.5 persons to each household.

83 As previously mentioned, the board limited B.C. producers to 71 birds on hand per quota right. Presumably this helped police restrictions more easily, but it surely reduced the productive efficiency of the industry still further. By how much we are not now prepared to even "guesstimate," but it surely will lead to more rapid flock turnover than is desirable, since older birds' laying rates are lower than younger birds. The Agricultural Economics Research Council of Canada's study, "The Cost of Canada's Egg System" (January 1979), has national data comparing Canada and the U.S., as well as regional U.S. data on flock size and production concentration for 1974. It suggests the same findings as in our Table III-1, though more dramatically. For example, in 1974, for the Western U.S., 94.7 percent of producers account for only 1.8 percent of the birds while 0.7 percent own 61.8 percent. In Canada, this report points out, only 20 producers have flock sizes over 50,000 hens and they account for only 10 percent of the egg market. For the U.S., these large operations account for 44 percent of the output. Interestingly, this study finds the characteristics of small producers in both countries to be the same, whereas larger firms are slightly more vertically integrated.

84 "An Examination of Egg Production Costs in Canada: A Report to the Canadian Egg Marketing Agency," January 1975.

85 There is the important exception of the very small sized operations where both Forbes *et al.* and Gary W. Dorosh, "The B.C. Egg Marketing Board: A Critical Evaluation" (extended M.A. essay submitted to the Department of Economics and Commerce, Simon Fraser University, August 1975), claim costs relative to higher output levels are understated.

86 Firms would have traded quota until their marginal production costs were equal. Some, actually many, would sell out completely and leave the industry. The important point to grasp is that if unit costs for the group could fall, they would fall as long as exchange of quota rights was not prohibited.

87 We merely multiplied the P.S. Ross estimates on Table III-2 by the output proportions for B.C. and Washington respectively. Thus, $54.9 = (.293) \cdot (51.5) + (.658) \cdot (54.8 + 56.0)/2 + (.049) \cdot (47.8)$, and $50.3 = (.029) \cdot (51.5) + (.317) \cdot (54.8 + 56.0)/2 + (.654) \cdot (47.8)$. Forbes *et al.* and, also, Gary Dorosh have argued, "The B.C. Egg Marketing Board: A Critical Evaluation," that the P.S. Ross estimates of

small or "family" egg farms underestimate cost, since many labour services, i.e., the opportunity cost of family members other than the household's head, are treated as free goods. Since such is patently wrong, the true difference between the industry's average costs is not 3.5 cents but something more.

88 The annual output for 1975 was 48.4 million dozens, including breakers. When this figure is multiplied by 3.6 cents, the $1.7 million savings emerges. Another piece of evidence that cost savings arise from scale expansion is the rapid increase in quota values over the last few years. A rise from around $400 or $500 per unit of quota in the early years of CEMA to $1,300 today (all adjusted to 1975 prices) is hard to explain on any other basis, since it is unlikely the industry anticipated future demand increases (the opposite is probably true) or technological changes lowering costs that were not foreseen in 1973. Further, it is unlikely that the ability to use the monopoly power inherent in its powers have increased. Forbes more recently, in his late 1977 "Brief to [the B.C.] Select Standing Committee on Agriculture," indicates eggs are priced only 8 cents (in 1975 prices) above their production cost, almost half his 1975 measure. This is hardly convincing, however, given the continual rise in quota prices with inflation effects removed. What has happened is that producers have been permitted to sell and to buy additional quota. The marginal viable firm may now grow to a 20,000 maximum from the previous high of 14,000. Since marginal cost is low and declining in that range, perhaps π has grown slightly, even given a greater reluctance of the BCEMB and CEMA to exercise their joint monopoly power overtly.

89 Table III-1 suggests that only 3 percent of the industry would look like the typical firm today with 140 units of quota; 32 percent of firms would each on average hold 400 units of quota, and the bulk of them would hold over 700 cases. Since a unit of quota allows the production of 30 dozen eggs per week, every week of the year (less 15 percent for effective marketing adjustment), the number of firms in each class is easily computed. With 48.4 million dozen eggs per year (36,000 cases of unadjusted quota), the numbers in each group are 7, 29, and 34 (from smallest to largest scale).

90 "On the Efficient Design of an Agricultural Marketing Board," Department of Economics, Carleton University, July 1975.

91 Actually, W_{R3} is slightly larger, since breakers under competitive conditions will also be produced, according to the ratio 4 to 96 of fresh (see Table III-3 in text below). Assuming a similar $\delta = 2.5$ cents, cost savings for these eggs yield an addition to W_{R2} of $5,000. Since W_{R1} was based on a breaker to shell ratio of 7 to 100, an empirical fact under monopoly, it meant our estimate of Q_m adjusted for breakers would be too high by 1.9 million eggs and, therefore, W_{R2} would be $6,000 too high. Since this more or less offsets the downward bias of $5,000, we have ignored them both in the text. The reason for the differences is the lower ratio of breakers

to fresh eggs in competition as opposed to monopoly. This is discussed below in the accompanying text.

92 The theoretics behind this fascinating hypothesis are discussed by George J. Stigler in "The Theory of Regulation," *Bell Journal of Economics* (Fall 1971).

93 *Report on Egg Prices* (Ottawa: 1975).

94 Richard Shaffner, "Canada's Import Quota on Eggs," claims that exports since 1973 were almost entirely breakers, "many" of them fresh eggs subject to CEMA's surplus removal. Forbes, "Brief to [the B.C.] Select Standing Committee on Agriculture," claims that CEMA no longer stores whole eggs purchased on surplus removal. They are sold to the breaker market or "exported at subsidized prices." Forbes, speaking for the CAC, claims that this was admitted to the Canadian Senate Agriculture Committee by CEMA management in Spring of 1977.

95 Shaffner, "Canada's Import Quota on Eggs."

96 GATT permits "import restrictions on any agricultural or fisheries product . . . necessary to the enforcement of governmental measures which operate to restrict quantities of the like domestic product to be marketed or produced."

97 Shaffner, "Canada's Import Quota on Eggs."

98 Tamek and Robinson, *Agricultural Product Prices*, and Whetstone, "A Free Market for Eggs." It should be noted that seconds or cracks are known as checks on the Chicago Mercantile Exchange, the leading forward market for shell and processed eggs in the U.S.

99 Twenty cents $\times$ 3 percent $\times$ 48.4 million dozens = $280,000. This assumes that $\sigma = \infty$. If we used $\sigma = 5.0$, this loss estimate would rise by less than $1,000.

100 The issue of surplus disposal and a measure of its importance are discussed for Australia by Beck, "The Social Cost of Production Control in the Australian Egg Industry." Beck finds for the period 1965-66 through 1972-73 that overproduction was 8 to 10 percent of the total retail value of domestic sales for Australia. Our estimates suggest it is slightly less than 1 percent for B.C. at the farm gate.

101 McManus, "On the Efficient Design of an Agricultural Marketing Board." Beck's study, "The Social Cost of Production in the Australian Egg Industry," does not appear to be an exception, since overproduction was financed in part by the government spreading the cost to some extent on general taxpayers; in other words, the difference between the marginal cost of fresh eggs and their lower realized price on international markets was made up by government subsidies. CEMA, on the other hand, has since 1975 been totally self-financing on its surplus disposal. Further, its early large losses appear to have been made up by later levies on producers according to perusal of their reports.

102　The discussion on quality effects of regulation is taken from conversations with John McManus and from his study, "On the Efficient Design of an Agricultural Marketing Board." He devotes an entire section to these two problems for both the broiler and egg markets. He cites among others two studies: Ontario Special Commission on Farm Income, *Marketing of Poultry and Eggs in Ontario*, Research Report No. 2 (1969), and L.E. Dawson and Ellen Bouwkamp, "Factors Affecting Flavor of Poultry Meat and Eggs," *World Poultry Science* (March 1969).

103　This follows since any one farmer's effect on market price of exceeding quota would be negligible. Thus, he or she will be sorely tempted to exceed allotted quota. Since the number of farms in existence exceeds that which would operate in free markets, the effect of not monitoring quota allotments would be costly price wars and a rapid movement back to the competitive price. It should also be clear that the intermediate buyers have a negative interest in quota maintenance.

104　This has to do with the diminished incentives that managers of collective organizations have as opposed to managers in profit oriented firms. There is a long literature on this, but the simplest accessible discussion is to be found in Armen A. Alchian, "Some Economics of Property Rights," in *Selected Works by Armen A. Alchian: Economic Forces at Work* (Indianapolis: Liberty Press, 1977). Readers of *The Journal of Law and Economics*, *The Bell Journal of Economics*, *The Journal of Economic Issues*, *Public Choice*, *The Journal of Political Economy*, *The American Economic Review*, *Economic Inquiry* and *The Canadian Journal of Economics* (to name the more prominent vehicles of this scholarly dissemination) will find abundant empirical evidence for this hypothesis.

105　Whetstone, "A Free Market for Eggs." Fisher cites this evidence, too, in "A Study of Agricultural Marketing."

106　Not all eggs would be of higher quality under a competitive regime, but more would be. This raises average quality, hence, demand-price offers. Of course, the price line would have to be adjusted upward, too, to take into account the extra "conversion costs" of higher quality shell eggs. Looking at only the areas above the price lines when considering quality essentially means we are assuming that producer rent changes are trivial. This would be the case if conversion costs were invariant to industry output. Since they are largely a function of mash-feed quality and hen age, inputs in virtually totally elastic supply, this is a reasonably accurate approximation of quality-supply conditions. On the measuring of surplus differences for quality alterations see Y. Barzel, "An Alternative Approach to the Analysis of Taxation," *Journal of Political Economy* (December 1976) and Barzel and Hall, *The Oil Import Quota*.

107 The reaction of American receivers of Canadian shell egg exports before and after the BCEMB and CEMA is an important piece of evidence we could not unearth. Casual discussions with grocery managers in Vancouver and Bellingham suggested there was no discernible difference in B.C.'s monopoly product and Washington State's competitive eggs. It could be that the consumer demand for "freshness" is sufficiently price inelastic to ensure that graders and wholesalers exert strong pressures on producers and that said pressure is backed up by marketing board supervision.

108 *The Citizen and the State: Essays on Regulation* (Chicago: University of Chicago Press, 1975). He is particularly articulate on this subject in his review of Galbraith's famous book, *American Capitalism* (Boston: Houghton-Mifflin, 1953), found in the *American Economic Review*, Supplement (May 1954).

109 A superior recent theoretical treatment of this is offered by Sam Peltzman, "Toward a More General Theory of Regulation," *Journal of Law and Economics* (August 1976). Two much less difficult analyses of the problem are found in Stigler, "The Theory of Regulation," *The Bell Journal of Economics and Management Science* (Spring 1971) and Richard A. Posner, "Regulation as Taxation" in that same issue. All of this is summarized by Posner in the second edition of his text, *Economic Analysis of Law* (Toronto: Little, Brown Canada, 1977). For an interesting, insightful, but descriptive treatment of U.S. monopoly creation in the New Deal see Hawley, *The New Deal and the Problem of Monopoly*, and Gabriel Kolko, *Railroads and Regulation 1877-1916* (New York: W.W. Norton and Co., 1970) for the earlier, post-*Munn* decision period.

110 As mentioned earlier in the text, Mark Twain noted a century ago in *Letters to the Earth* that although free-traders had both logic and general welfare on their side, protectionists got the votes in Congress. That these votes were localized special interests and not for some national purpose is supported by Jonathan J. Pincus, "Pressure Groups and the Pattern of Tariffs," *Journal of Political Economy* (August 1975). Per capita stakes are small for the large, diverse group but very high for the smaller, cohesive coalition. Cost of organizing both of them and getting across the requisite information is such that it does not pay to block much uneconomic legislation. Economic illiteracy cannot be completely dismissed, however, as another source of misallocation. If this were the only cause, however, we would not predict the regularities in tariff and monopoly creation we, in fact, observe. We suspect both influences are at work: informed self-interest on the part of cohesive groups and ignorance of such on the part of the general population. That there is a limit to the former's ability to exploit the latter, frequently set at less than full monopoly returns, is shown by Peltzman, "Toward a More General Theory of Regulation."

111 Robert A. Ippolito and Richard I. Masson, "The Social Cost of Federal Regulation of Milk," Antitrust Division, U.S. Department

of Justice (January 1976). A version of this paper is found in the *Journal of Law and Economics* (April 1978). They do not, unfortunately, have a measure of the political organization costs borne by the losers, consumers of fresh milk, in attempting to mitigate or defeat the efforts of producers. Their estimate is, thus, a lower bounded one.

112   The reader should carefully distinguish the difference between resources devoted to seeking monopoly rents and those used to increase producer rents by monopoly privileges. The latter is the correct measure of the value of monopoly to producers, since it nets out from monopoly rents losses realized in (a) reduced producer surplus and (b) organization inefficiencies due to contraction of competitive output. Ippolito and Masson, "The Social Cost of Federal Regulation of Milk," have this right, but Grubel and Schwindt, *The Real Cost of the B.C. Milk Board*, neglect these offsets.

113   See notes 39 and 42 and the text to which they refer.

114   48.4 million dozen $\times$ 35 percent of 4.25 cents = \$0.7 million.

115   Posner, "The Social Cost of Monopoly and Regulation," cites 10 percent as the total social loss for milk in the U.S., using Ippolito and Masson's data in their "The Social Cost of Federal Regulation of Milk."

116   The "Theory of Second Best" will not rescue proponents of marketing boards. Briefly, the latter say that, if there are distortions elsewhere, a distortion in agriculture might be welfare correcting. Second-best is a marginal concept, however, and the bulk of the social costs of monopoly are, as we have shown, dissipations of the nontriangle, large rectangle type. We believe the second best problem, therefore, is probably of totally trivial consequence. On this see Harberger, "On Measuring the Social Opportunity Cost of Labor," *International Labour Review* (June 1971), and Kochin, "The Social Cost of Union Gains," *Statsvetenskpalig Tidskrift* 5 (1980).

117   It appears as if much political power has already been lost by agricultural interests in the U.S. See the essays in Martin E. Abel *et al.*, *Food and Agricultural Policy* (Washington, D.C., American Enterprise Institute for Public Policy Research, 1977).

118   These coefficients of variations are the standard deviation of monthly prices within a year, divided by the mean of the prices for the year. It is one simple way of comparing variation between disparate groups of data.

119   Before the BCEMB the coefficient of variation (1964 through 1968) averaged 10.7 percent for B.C. and 11.2 percent for Washington; hardly a difference. For the post-BCEMB, pre-CEMA period (1969 through 1972), Washington State's coefficient of variation rose to 19.8 percent and B.C.'s fell to 5.9 percent. Since CEMA, the

average is 14.0 percent for Washington State and 5.8 percent for B.C. If 1973 is taken out as a "disorderly" year for Canada, given the anticipation of CEMA and the overstocking by egg farmers of layers in 1972, CEMA could be said to have reduced the price dispersion still more, though so few data points are involved that we reluctantly offer the respective average of dispersion for the period (1974 through 1977) as 13.3 and 4.3 percent respectively.

120   A distinguished Chicago economist, D. Gale Johnson, *Forward Prices for Agriculture* (Chicago: University of Chicago Press, 1947), recognizes that capital intensity and entrepreneurship are negatively affected by risk. He suggested that the government estimate these future contingencies and guarantee a significant fraction of this price at the time of sale on the spot market. Needless to say, the government must be a better guesser than the futures market for this to work out. Further as he later pointed out in "Government and Agriculture: Is Agriculture a Special Case," *Journal of Law and Economics* (October 1958), the pressure on the government to estimate generous prices to farmers would be significant, leading to excessive production and large and wasteful subsidies. The U.S. agriculture program with its guarantees and its parity notions is a case in point. See T. Dudley Wallace on various U.S. programs, "Measures of Social Cost of Agricultural Programs."

121   In 1920 over one-third of Canada's population was in agriculture, whereas in 1976 less than one-twentieth was found there (McConnell and Pope, *Economics: First Canadian Edition*). In the U.S. that change has been even more dramatic. In 1920 almost three in ten persons lived on farms; today that number has fallen to less than one in twenty-five. U.S. Department of Commerce, Bureau of the Census, *Statistical Abstract of the U.S.*, 98th ed. (Washington, D.C.: U.S. Government Printing Office, 1978).

122   Reuben A. Kessel, "A Study of the Effects of Competition in the Tax Exempt Bond Market," *Journal of Political Economy* (July/ August 1971), argues that an industry with eight suppliers of which the four largest firms supply no more than three-fifths the output is, for all intents and purposes, very competitive. Agro-business in its concentrated extremes would easily fall well within these limits, especially so when foreign suppliers are considered.

123   For the U.S., D. Gale Johnson cites in "Government and Agriculture: Is Agriculture a Special Case?" that measures of income generally understate real farm incomes by 25 percent. McConnell and Pope, *Economics: First Canadian Edition*, present evidence that farm operators have done as well as the average Canadian over time, though poor farmers certainly do exist. Those who subscribe to the theory that over the long pull farmers earn less than normal returns are unwittingly offering an hypothesis of rural incompetence. Post-Granger movement politics in the U.S. and Canada are totally at variance with this view of bucolic ignorance.

124   But this subsidy must be independent of output. We do not wish to advocate a subsidy on fresh eggs, which would lead to too many being consumed. Unfortunately, as a practical matter, almost any but a once-and-for-all subsidy will do this.

125   R.M.A. Loyns and W.F. Lu, "Characteristics of Demand for Eggs in Canada," show that the income elasticity for fresh eggs is 0.05. (Hassan and Johnson's estimate in "The Demand for Major Foods in Canada" is still lower, 0.01. We will use Loyns and Lu's estimate, as it yields a slightly less regressive tax schedule.) In 1975, the average B.C. family consumed almost 68 dozen fresh eggs and had an income around $20,000 before taxes. Had it received half that income it would have consumed at least 66 dozen (more actually, since after tax income would not be halved). Should its income have risen four times to $80,000, it would have consumed no more than 73 dozen (less because of progressive taxes). Given a monopoly mark-up of 11 cents per dozen, the tax rate on income is 0.07 percent for the poorest family in our example, 0.03 percent for the middle income household, and 0.01 percent for the richest family.

126   Recently economists have questioned whether examples of inequality creating implicit taxes are merely misguided, ill-informed efforts, or deliberate attempts to make worse off the bottom group in society so as to subsidize the more affluent classes. Evidence is mounting that the chief net beneficiaries of government are the middle classes, and the losers are the poor and the wealthy. On this see Gordon Tullock, "The Charity of the Uncharitable," *Western Economic Journal* (December 1971). Recently W. Irwin Gillespie, *In Search of Robin Hood* (Montreal: C.D. Howe Institute, 1978), has made the same point using Canadian data. This theme, together with dramatized evidence, is vigorously put forth by Nobel laureate Milton Friedman in his current (U.S.) Public Broadcasting Television series, "Free to Choose." The arguments are explored at some length in his nontechnical book co-authored with his wife, Rose, *Free to Choose: A Personal Statement* (New York: Harcourt Brace Jovanovich, Inc., 1980).

127   Harberger finds the average deadweight burden of the U.S. income tax around 15 percent of revenue collected ("Taxation, Resource Allocation and Welfare," in *Taxation and Welfare*). Recently, however, Edgar K. Browning, "The Marginal Cost of Public Funds," *Journal of Political Economy* (April 1976), has recalculated this, looking at the marginal deadweight of this tax and including collection expenses, to be 20 to 30 percent. Even at this higher cost, 25 to 30 cents of waste per dollar transferred would be saved by employing the fiscal instead of regulatory redistribution systems.

128   In everyday parlance we are asking whether the loss is the result of what businessmen and lawyers call "normal business risk." It is hard to tell. On average, investors think that the monopoly will last from eight to twenty years. This is the period of time necessary to pay off a $1,000 quota, at 8 to 12 percent borrowing rates, that yields

a mark-up of 10 to 15 cents per dozen above production costs. Of course, there is a probability distribution of durabilities around this eight- to twenty-year average. The theory of "rational expectations" asserts that such possibilities will be taken into account by rational investors. With no objective means of determining what the expectations are of each level of durability, one could not comment *ex post* on whether the market's assessment was correct or not.

129 Harry G. Johnson once remarked in private conversation that the reason compensation is not paid to lower a tariff or remove some other state erected barrier is that the general citizenry would view it as tribute or blackmail. That means in many cases that society is "stuck" with a misallocation, since, without compensation, there can be no means of achieving acquiescence of the disadvantaged.

130 One interesting discussion of the takings issue is found in Bruce Ackerman, *Private Property and the Constitution* (New Haven: Yale University Press, 1977). Borcherding and Jack Knetsch, "Expropriation of Private Property and the Basis for Compensation," *The University of Toronto Law Journal* (Summer 1979), address the question of compensation for takings where the asset expropriated for public benefit has a "legitimate" private use.

131 Maryon Brechin, "Marketing Boards: CAC's View," *Canadian Consumer* (June 1977).

132 The July issue of *Consumer Report*, a publication of the CAC's sister organization in the U.S., the American Consumers' Union (ACU), supported the recall of children's sleepwear treated with the flame retardent, Tris. This was because of Tris's alleged carcinogenic hazard, though (a) Tris was originally introduced at the behest of the U.S. Consumer Products' Safety Commission and was supported by the ACU; (b) the cost of recall would be over $200 million; (c) the risk of cancer for a child wearing freshly treated sleepwear every evening for several years is no more than three in one-hundred thousand for male children and less for females; and (d) Tris quickly washes out over time. *Consumer Reports* has opted for safety and against low cost fire protection, a subtle but subjective trade-off. On what poll of their members did they base this judgement? None that we know of. Their support of the saccharin ban is an example where they have opted for a "tax" on diabetics and the obese to "subsidize" the health of the rest of the public. Again, value judgements have been made involving conflicting interests among consumers. Ralph Nader's "consumerist" positions are so well-known and so controversial that further discussion is hardly necessary. Still it is well to recall that no mechanism of public choice even approaching the crudities of community majority rule legitimize his various positions.

133 Posner's "Regulation by Taxation" surveys this problem. He shows that the regulators do not pursue the public interest because of difficulties in assessing it and because the politics of specialized

interests are dominant. He especially concentrates on the discriminatory price and rate structures that regulation almost always creates, leading to massive cross-subsidies to the politically advantaged at the expense of the more diffuse group.

134 That nonprofit agencies, public and private, have a Parkinsonian interest in supplying more of their product to the community than is desirable is well-known among students of bureaucracy. See essays in Thomas E. Borcherding (ed.), *Budgets and Bureaucrats* (Durham, North Carolina: Duke University Press, 1977).

135 The case of the open cartel which dissipates all or a great deal of the monopoly rents while still raising consumer price above competitive levels is found as an exercise in the late Henry C. Simons' study notes, *Economics 201 Syllabus* (mimeograph, University of Chicago Bookstore, no date). This discussion is readily available, however, in Don Patinkin, "Multiple-Plant Firms, Cartels and Imperfect Competition," *Quarterly Journal of Economics* (February 1947).

136 The noneconomist reader is advised to read *Regulation: The American Enterprise Institution's Journal on Government and Society*. The first issue, (July/August 1977) surveys the cost of market regulation in the U.S. Kristol's discussion, "A Regulated Society?" is contained therein. Technical economists need to look no further than the last ten years' issues of almost any of the leading economic journals, but in particular the *Journal of Law and Economics* and the *Bell Journal of Economics*, to find massive evidence attesting to the cost of regulation. We are tempted to say that, excepting unemployment and inflation, regulatory distortions have replaced the tariff as the *bête noir* of North American economists.

Index

RECENT RELEASES

REACTION: THE NATIONAL ENERGY PROGRAM

Some of the most talked about and highly controversial issues facing Canada today are energy supply, pricing, and the question of how the resource income pie is to be shared. In the Fall of 1980, the federal government released its National Energy Program (NEP) and its objectives are as follows:

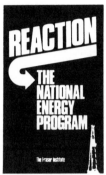

● To establish the basis for Canadians to seize control of their own energy through **security** of supply and ultimate independence from the world oil market.

● To offer to Canadians, all Canadians, the real **opportunity** to participate in the energy industry in general and the petroleum industry in particular, and to share the benefits of industry expansion.

● To establish a petroleum pricing and revenue-sharing regime that recognizes the requirement of **fairness** to all Canadians no matter where they live.

In response to the government's program, the Fraser Institute has published this timely and thought-provoking critique — a candid assessment of the aims and implications of the program. Written by some of Canada's most highly-regarded economists, the authors analyze the steps the government proposes to take in order to achieve its started objectives.

In their conclusions the authors indicate that the National Energy Program should be regarded as a **first draft** rather than a final, immutable policy of government. They also suggest that Canadians should carefully reconsider their support of the program in its present form.

Contributors to this highly relevant critique include: **Thomas J. Courchene** (University of Western Ontario), **John A. G. Grant** (Wood Gundy Limited), **Kenneth H. Norrie** (University of Alberta), and **Daryll G. Waddingham** and **John G. Stabback** (Royal Bank of Canada). Mr. Stabback was formerly Chairman of the National Energy Board. Editors are **G. Campbell Watkins** (DataMetrics Limited) and **Michael A. Walker** (Fraser Institute).

166 pages   3 figures   22 tables $6.95 paperback   ISBN 0-88975-042-4

UNIONS AND THE PUBLIC INTEREST
Collective Bargaining in the Government Sector

In this book, **Sandra Christensen**, an economist at Simon Fraser University, examines the growth and development of public sector unions. Professor Christensen provides a useful analysis of the determination of public sector rates of pay and offers provocative but practical suggestions for ways to cope with dispute resolutions.

SOME HIGHLIGHTS OF THE BOOK

● One out of five people in the active work force is employed in the government sector and nine tenths of them are unionized.

● Nearly half of total union membership is employed by governments and public administration is the most heavily unionized of all the major sectors in the economy.

● The extent to which compensation in the public sector exceeds that in the private sector ranges as high as 30 per cent and averages about nine per cent excluding a consideration of shorter work week, longer vacation entitlement, superior pension and employment stability in the public sector.

● Legislation governing public employees in Canada is more liberal than the legislation prevailing in either the United States or the United Kingdom.

● Wages in the public sector should be set according to the "prevailing wage" principle on the basis of comparability with the private sector.

● Since many public services have been given an exclusive monopoly by government legislation, collective bargaining over wages in the governmental sector means that the principle of the prevailing wage is replaced by a system of public ransom.

● The responsibility for pay strikes in the public sector rests with the legislation that permits such strikes. Having given unions the power to engage in these activities there should be no surprise that they use it enthusiastically.

If you are concerned about the relative power of public sector unions and the public sector's role in the wage spiral, this book is must reading for you.

95 pages   11 tables bibliography $5.95 paperback   ISBN 0-88975-022-X

RENT CONTROL: MYTHS AND REALITIES
International Evidence of the Effects
of Rent Control in Six Countries

Drawing on experiences in six countries over the last 50 years, a group of economists, including Nobel Prize Winners **Friedrich Hayek** and **Milton Friedman,** discuss the myth and the reality of rent control. The authors present definitive evidence that, in the final analysis, "there is no case for control."

Other contributors to this Fraser Institute critique of rent control include **George Stigler** (University of Chicago), **Bertrand de Jouvenel** (SEDEIS, Bureau of Economic Research, Paris), **F. W. Paish** (University of London), **F. G. Pennance** (late of the University of Aberdeen), **Sven Rydenfelt** (University of Lund, Sweden), **Michael A. Walker** (Fraser Institute), **Frank Kristof** (Rent Stabilization Association of New York City), **Basil A. Kalymon** (University of Toronto), **Ted Dienstfrey** (California Housing Council), **Richard Ault** (Louisiana State University), and Editors **Walter Block** (Fraser Institute) and **Edgar O. Olsen** (University of Virginia).

A surprising feature of this book is that a group of economists of a variety of ideological persuasions comes to a unanimous conclusion about the effects of rent control.

256 pages $7.95 paperback   ISBN 0-88975-033-5

Fraser Institute/Order Form

Books on Current Economic Issues

___ REACTION: THE NATIONAL ENERGY PROGRAM .... $ 6.95

___ TAX FACTS .... $ 3.95

___ PRIVATIZATION:THEORY & PRACTICE $12.95

___ THE HEALTH CARE BUSINESS .... $ 5.95

___ CANADIAN CONFEDERATION AT THE CROSSROADS .... $ 9.95

___ THE SCIENCE COUNCIL'S WEAKEST LINK .... $ 4.95

___ OIL IN THE SEVENTIES .... $ 9.95

___ FRIEDMAN ON GALBRAITH .... $ 3.95

___ WHICH WAY AHEAD? .... $ 4.95

___ THE ILLUSION OF WAGE & PRICE CONTROL .... $ 2.95

___ MINORITY RIGHTS & WRONGS .... $ 5.95

___ THE EGG MARKETING BOARD .... $ 3.95

Housing & Land Economic Series

___ RENT CONTROL: MYTHS & REALITIES .... $ 7.95

___ ZONING .... $ 4.95

___ PUBLIC PROPERTY? .... $ 9.95

___ ANATOMY OF A CRISIS .... $ 3.95

___ PROFITS IN THE REAL ESTATE INDUSTRY .... $ 2.95

___ THE DO'S AND DON'TS OF HOUSING POLICY .... $ 8.00

Labour Market Series

___ UNEMPLOYMENT INSURANCE $14.95

___ UNIONS AND THE PUBLIC INTEREST .... $ 5.95

The Fraser Institute
626 Bute Street, Vancouver, B.C.
Canada V6E 3M1
(604) 688-0221

Total # of books: _____ Sub-total: $ _____

Postage/handling (per order): **$1.00**

Total : $ _____

☐ Cheque/money order payable to **The Fraser Institute** enclosed

☐ Charge my credit card   Visa ☐   Mastercharge ☐

Card #: _____ Expires: /

Signature: _____

Name (print): _____

Organization: _____

Address: _____

City: _____ Prov./State: _____ Code: _____

Please send me information about membership in The Fraser Institute ☐

10/80